Sunrise of Power

Ancient Egypt

Alexander and the World of
Hellenism

Empires

Their Rise and Fall

Sunrise of Power

Ancient Egypt

Alexander and the World of Hellenism

Joyce Milton

Preface by William Kelly Simpson,
Professor of Egyptology, Yale University;
Curator of Egyptian and Ancient Near Eastern Art
Museum of Fine Arts, Boston

Boston Publishing Company, Inc.
Boston, Massachusetts

Empires: Their Rise and Fall is published in the United States by Boston Publishing Company, Inc., and distributed by Field Publications.

Author, Joyce Milton
Picture Researcher, Janet Adams
Assistant Picture Researcher, Noreen O'Gara
Translator, Ilana D'Ancona
Historical Consultant, William Kelly Simpson
Project Consultant, Valerie Hopkins
Design Implementation, Designworks

Boston Publishing Company, Inc.

President, Robert J. George
Editor-In-Chief, Robert Manning
Managing Editor, Paul Dreyfus
Marketing Director, Jeanne Gibson

Field Publications

President, Bruce H. Seide
Publisher, Marilyn Black
Marketing Director, Kathleen E. Long

Rizzoli Editore

Authors of the Italian Edition:
  Introduction: Professor Ovidio Dallera
  Egypt: Dr. Flavio Conti
  Hellenism: Dr. Giampaolo Polvani and Dr. Giorgio Bombi
  Maps: Fernando Russo
Idea and Realization, Harry C. Lindinger
Graphic Design, Gerry Valsecchi
General Editorial Supervisor, Ovidio Dallera

© 1986 by Rizzoli Editore
Printed in the United States

Library of Congress Catalog Card Number: 79-53139
ISBN: 0-15-004024-5

Field Publications offers handsome bookends and other decorative desk items. For information, write to:
Field Publications, P.O. Box 16617, Columbus, Ohio 43216.

Contents

Preface   7

Ancient Egypt   9

The fortunes of the Nile   18
The power of the written word   20
Bread and beer   30
The common man   32
The army in parade and action   40
Egyptian women and the sisterhood   48
Egyptian beauty rites   50
Atenism   52
Life and afterlife   60
Medicinal magic   62
A god for any occasion   72
Holy animals   74
Funeral customs   84

Alexander and the World of Hellenism   89

The myth of Alexander   96
The long march   100
Battle of the Granicus   104
Battle of Issus   112
Battle of Gaugamela   118
Greco-Oriental art   132
The kingdom after Alexander   136
Antigonus the One-Eyed   137
The Seleucids   137
Ptolemy   137
Flax monopoly   146
Weights and measures   147
Encounter with Rome   148
Pergamon   154
Hellenistic art and the grotesque   160
Gold work   162

Photography credits   170
Index   171

Preface

The history of civilized man, from about 3000 B.C. to the present, represents only a fraction of human life on earth. Yet we are heirs to a most diverse and disparate succession of empires, kingdoms, and peoples. The achievements of man in forming a world of nations in cooperation—if not always at peace—have not been easily won. Man's inhumanity to man looms large in any view of the past: warfare, enslavement, the destruction of people, the burning of cities and farms, torture, and imprisonment—all these the chronicles relate and even sometimes boast of.

And this mania for self-destruction has been vented on man's noblest creations. The celebrated library of Alexandria was burned to the ground, destroying the world's greatest collection of scientific and literary works. Few are the temples and palaces still standing in Greece and Egypt, and every one a ruin of its former grandeur. And in the relatively enlightened climate of the present day, the destruction continues. In the past, monuments were violated by barbarian hordes; today they are prey to the exigencies of a growing global population. The spread of the cities and the concomitant need to extend agricultural land by irrigation necessitate the destruction of archaeological sites around the world. Even the pyramids of Egypt have been set aside as quarries for building stones and lime for the kilns, while settlement debris provides a ready source for fertilizer.

Under the circumstances, it is remarkable how much of ancient societies—their thought and literature, their monuments and artworks—remains. For the earliest civilizations, our knowledge begins with scanty, often mythological, lists of kings. In the temples of ancient Egypt, the prowess of the king is dramatized in battle, in receiving tributes of the vanquished, and in other ennobling pursuits that glorify his reign. The greater part of the scenes and texts represented in the temples, however, illustrates and describes the rituals performed by the king for the gods. He is shown over and over again making offerings to the god, burning incense, opening the god's shrine—engaged in innumerable cultic acts.

Although the Egyptian kings are identified by name, their personalities rarely rise above their activities. It is as though an individual is cast in a familiar play, in which he obediently assumes the stock role of king or noble. There are actually cases where one king has simply removed the name of an earlier king to insert his own without otherwise changing the scene or text. So, too, the representations of Alexander the Great in Egyptian temples are indistinguishable from those of his predecessors and followers. In the Greek and Macedonian chronicles, on the other hand, Alexander's conquests are treated as the single-handed accomplishment of one outstanding man. The histories of the Hellenistic kingdoms that grew out of his empire are filled with the wars, jealousies, and confusing alliances of the *diadochi,* Alexander's successors, but information about the day-to-day lives of the people—bureaucrats and merchants, soldiers and scholars, peasants and slaves—is meager.

Yet beneath the impression of cold anonymity, glimpses of individuals do emerge. Officials of Old Kingdom Egypt describe their expeditions to the quarries and their participation in caravan journeys. Harkhuf of the Sixth Dynasty brings back a dancing dwarf to his child patron, King Pepi II. The father of King Merikare of the First Intermediate Period gives pragmatic and often bitter advice to his son on the treatment of courtiers. Akhenaten and Nefertiti are shown in paintings fondling and kissing their beloved infant daughters. Piankhi, the black Sudanese who was an ardent equestrian, is aghast to discover how his enemy's horses have suffered as the result of one of his sieges.

In contrast, the literature and documents of Hellenistic society reveal a more complex society. The polyglot atmosphere of the cosmopolis not only gave rise to many tensions (some of the first examples of anti-Semitic writing appear in Hellenistic Egypt) but also fostered an environment that must have been both lively and stimulating. The plays of the Athenian Menander, for example, speak of citizens from a wide variety of classes and ethnic backgrounds who converge in the streets of Alexandria, exchanging quips about their respective Greek accents and falling in love with strangers whom they must contrive to meet.

So it was that the new Macedonian dynasties in Greece, Syria, and Mesopotamia by slow degrees transformed the Western world, creating the new order of Hellenism. The legacies of Greece, Palestine and the Levant, Mesopotamia, and Egypt were incorporated into this new order. And then, gradually in some areas and suddenly in others, the Western world received a new master: Imperial Rome.

WILLIAM KELLY SIMPSON
Professor of Egyptology, Yale University

Ancient Egypt

Today's rulers could find much to envy in the lives of the pharaohs. In a world where temporal power is always vulnerable and frequently short-lived, it is sobering to recall the serene confidence of the Egyptian god-kings, whose power was absolute even in death. Nor did they doubt the permanence of their kingdom on earth. Having no historical models for the rise and fall of empires, the ancient Egyptians had every reason to believe that their civilization would last forever—and they weren't far wrong.

The kingdom that called itself the Two Lands endured for two and a half millennia. When it finally collapsed, it left behind a vast store of antiquities that has fascinated—and often perplexed—the world ever

since. Greek and Roman travelers marveled at the temples of the Nile, leaving graffiti on the walls of monuments that were already as ancient in their eyes as the Parthenon and the Roman Forum are in ours. Beginning with the Renaissance, crazes for Egyptian artifacts periodically swept Europe. In 1833, a French monk, Father Géramb, noted that "it would hardly be respectable, on one's return from Egypt, to present oneself in Europe without a mummy in one hand and a crocodile in the other."

Egyptomania has not always contributed to a deeper understanding of the people of the Nile. Roman emperors enthusiastically carried off the obelisks raised by their Egyptian predecessors, while Roman scholars were content to speculate about the meaning of the hieroglyphs carved on the Egyptian imports. Though hieroglyphic writing was used by Egyptian priests through Ptolemaic times, Herodotus made no attempt to record its basic principles, and Pliny the Elder merely suggested that the inscriptions comprised "an account of natural science. . . ."

Pliny's suggestion marked the beginning of a series of exaggerated claims made for Egyptian science, both practical and occult, based on signs and symbols whose meaning was completely misinterpreted. Alchemists, magicians, and members of secret societies published spurious "dictionaries" of hieroglyphs, and

Egypt's reputation as a fount of esoteric knowledge was finally sealed by an international fad that promoted powdered mummy as a health cure. Enterprising speculators and travelers happily joined in the plunder of ancient tombs. One sixteenth-century Scotsman, John Sanderson, was lucky enough to purchase no less than six hundred pounds of assorted mummy parts in Memphis which he then sold in the British Isles at the going rate of eight shillings per pound.

Napoleon Bonaparte, who saw Egypt as fertile ground for an empire rather than as a cache of ancient booty, was one of the first to put the study of ancient Egypt on a more serious footing. On his 1798 expedition to the Nile, Napoleon took along 175 French savants who set about making accurate drawings of Egyptian monuments, including many which have since been destroyed. But the most important contribution to future scholarship was made by Captain Bouchard, a French officer responsible for digging fortifications for Fort Rachid in the Nile Delta. It was one of his men who uncovered a stele of black basalt covered with a text copied in three distinct alphabets. Bouchard's discovery, later named the Rosetta stone after the nearby delta town, proved to be the long-sought key to hieroglyphic writing.

With the deciphering of the Rosetta stone, volumes of superstitious nonsense written about the Egyptians and their puzzling arcana suddenly became obsolete. Replacing the myths with an accurate historical record, however, was another matter. Given the ancient Egyptians' cyclic approach to dating, whereby each king's accession to the Throne of Horus marked the first year of a new cycle, even seemingly straightforward questions of chronology were wildly controversial. For example, Jean-François Champollion, who

Unaware of the Nile's true sources, the first farmers in the valley imagined that its yearly floods welled up from hidden caverns beneath the Nubian desert (left). Today this territory is the site of Lake Nasser, a vast reservoir created by the Aswan High Dam.

The Nile's progress through a virtually rainless land (facing page) creates stark contrasts. The Red Land, or djeseret (above right), was regarded by the ancients as a hostile force. Actually, it formed an effective buffer against invasion. Date palms and grain fields near Luxor (below right) are cultivated much in the ancient manner. The distinctive black color, or kemit, of the Nile's damp, fertile silt gave rise to the Egyptians' name for their country: the Black Land.

EARLY DYNASTIC PERIOD

3200–2780 B.C.

1st Dynasty (3200–2980)
2nd Dynasty (2980–2780)

The Rulers
Menes-Narmer / Aha / Djer / Den / Peribsen

Civil Events
Unification of Upper and Lower Egypt under one king. Development of funerary architecture and of building capabilities in general. Foundation of Memphis at the junction of Lower and Upper Egypt. Development of hieroglyphic writing and effective government.

Military Events
Campaigns against the Nubians and extension of Egyptian territory beyond the First Cataract.

☐ Capitals

● Major Cities and Monuments

LOWER EGYPT

■ BUTO

■ MEMPHIS

● Gerza

UPPER

● Badari

■ THINIS

EGYPT ● Nagada

HIERAKONPOLIS ■

First Cataract

THE OLD KINGDOM

2780–2258 B.C.

3rd Dynasty (2780–2680)
4th Dynasty (2680–2565)
5th Dynasty (2565–2420)
6th Dynasty (2420–2258)

The Rulers
Djoser / Snefru / Khufu / Khafre / Menkaure / Weserkaf / Sahure / Unas / Pepi I / Pepi II

Civil Events
Building of the first great stone structure under Djoser. Construction of the Great Pyramids at Giza by Khufu, and the carving of the Great Sphinx under Khafre, testifying to a high level of artistic and technical activity, a sound economic state, and a powerful central government. Trade throughout the East is intensified. The first religious texts are drawn on a monumental scale in tombs. Toward the end of the period, the provincial centers grow to be independent focuses of power, and Egypt undergoes a process of "feudalization," which weakens the pharaoh's authority.

Military Events
Forays into Nubia, Libya, Lebanon, Sinai, and Punt for raw materials. Sahure's punitive expedition by sea against Byblos. Military actions under Pepi I against tribes in both Sinai and Palestine.

LOWER EGYPT

Giza ● ● Heliopolis
Saqqara ● ■ MEMPHIS
● Dahshûr
Medum ● ■ HERACLEOPOLIS

UPPER

Abydos ●
EGYPT ● Coptos

NUBIA *First Cataract*

FIRST INTERMEDIATE PERIOD

2258–2040 B.C.

7th Dynasty (Memphis)
8th Dynasty (Memphis)
9th Dynasty (Heracleopolis)
10th Dynasty (Heracleopolis)

The Rulers
Khety I / Khety II / Merikare / Mentuhotep I

Civil Events
Collapse of central government and increase of power of provincial nomes. Local dynasties are formed at Memphis and Heracleopolis. The Heracleopolitan ruler prevails. Political turmoil; pyramids ransacked; social and political chaos. New despairing literary works are written, such as "Instructions for King Merikare" and "Dialogue of a Man Tired of Living with his Soul."

Military Events
Frequent wars among the various nome leaders for predominance. Incursions and forays from the Near East.

LOWER EGYPT

MEMPHIS ■

■ HERACLEOPOLIS

UPPER

■ ABYDOS
EGYPT ■ COPTOS

First Cataract

NUBIA

THE MIDDLE KINGDOM

2040–1786 B.C.

11th Dynasty
12th Dynasty

The Rulers
Mentuhotep II / Amenemmes I / Sesostris I / Amenemmes II / Sesostris II / Sesostris III / Amenemmes III / Amenemmes IV / Queen Sebekneferura

Civil Events
Reunification of Egypt by Mentuhotep II under the Theban house. Building of monumental tombs and temples on the eastern Nile shore opposite Thebes is begun. New capital established near Memphis, in a central location between the Two Lands. Reorganization of administration and centralization of power. The god Amon becomes predominant. Classical period of literature. Unprecedented prosperity, particularly under Sesostris III and Amenemmes III.

Military Events
Expeditions to Nubia, Libya, Sinai, and Syria initiated by Mentuhotep II. Military campaign against Palestine and complete conquest of Nubia under Sesostris III.

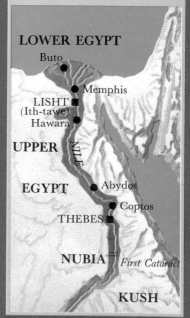

LOWER EGYPT

● Buto

● Memphis

LISHT ■
(Ith-tawe)
Hawara ●

UPPER

● Abydos
EGYPT ● Coptos

THEBES ●

NUBIA *First Cataract*

KUSH

SECOND INTERMEDIATE PERIOD

1786–1570 B.C.

13th Dynasty } (1786–1680)
14th Dynasty }
15th Dynasty } (1720–1570)
16th Dynasty } (Hyksos)
17th Dynasty   (1600–1570)

The Rulers
Hyksos: Salitis / Khian / Apopi I
Egyptians: Seqenenre II / Kamose

Civil Events
Repetitious dynastic crises and complete disintegration of central power. Collapse and impoverishment of the country. Chaotic situation created by invasion of the Hyksos from Asia. Rebirth of national feeling and revolt against Hyksos. Nubia and Lower Sudan take advantage of state of affairs in Egypt and regain independence. Introduction of the horse-drawn chariot.

Military Events
Hyksos conquer Lower Egypt and establish their rule there. Military campaigns conducted against the Hyksos by the Theban king Seqenenre II, who dies in battle. Kamose penetrates to Avaris, the Hyksos capital, and pursues his antagonists to Palestine. The end of Hyksos rule is in sight, and the way is cleared for the glories in arms and arts that marked the New Kingdom.

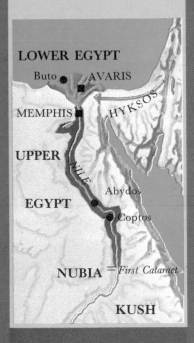

THE NEW KINGDOM

1570–1085 B.C.

18th Dynasty (1570–1342)
19th Dynasty (1342–1197)
20th Dynasty (1197–1085)

The Rulers
Ahmose I / Amenhotep I / Thutmose I / Thutmose II / Hatshepsut / Thutmose III / Amenhotep II / Thutmose IV / Amenhotep III / Amenhotep IV (Akhenaten) / Tutankhamon / Horemheb / Rameses I-Seti I / Rameses II / Merenptah / Rameses III

Civil Events
Crushing of Hyksos power in delta by Ahmose and the third unification of Egypt. Far-reaching military success leads to the rise of Egypt as a world power. Organized rule of conquered territories, and extensive trade with foreign cultures. Rule of Queen Hatshepsut, who declares herself king, builds Deir-el-Bahri temple. Amenhotep III builds the Luxor temple. Religious upheaval created by Akhenaten centered around the worship of the sun god Aten; a new capital is built; ultimate failure of the reform. Reign of Tutankhamon. Rameses III the last great pharaoh of Egypt.

Military Events
Ahmose's expeditions into Syria and Nubia to regain territory; Thutmose I reconquers Nubia. The campaigns, victories, and extensive conquests of Thutmose III. Palestine and Syria become Egyptian provinces. Frontier extended south to the Fourth Cataract. The east revolts during Akhenaten's reign. Rameses I and II organize campaigns to reconquer Palestine and Syria. Famous battle of Kadesh, with dubious outcome, between Egypt under Rameses II and the Hittites. The Sea Peoples threaten an invasion at the Nile Delta but are defeated by Rameses III.

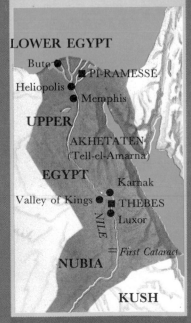

THIRD INTERMEDIATE PERIOD

1085–715 B.C.

21st Dynasty (1085–950)
22nd Dynasty (950–730)
23rd Dynasty (817–730)
24th Dynasty (730–715)

The Rulers
Smendes / Herihor / Sheshonq / Pedibast / Tef-nekht / Bakenrenef

Civil Events
End of Egyptian unity. Pharaohs are of foreign extraction. Independent principalities proliferate: Toward the middle of the eighth century B.C., four local sovereigns call themselves "pharaoh." Burials of the great New Kingdom pharaohs removed to a cache at Deir-el-Bahri to guard against widespread tomb robbing. Loss of Nubia and the decline of the empire in Asia.

Military Events
Sheshonq enters Palestine and plunders Jerusalem. The Kushites (Ethiopians) invade Upper Egypt.

THE LATE KINGDOM

715–332 B.C.

25th Dynasty (751–656) (Kushite)
26th Dynasty (663–525)
27th Dynasty (525–404) (Persian)
28th Dynasty (404–398)
29th Dynasty (398–378)
30th Dynasty (378–341)
31st Dynasty (341–332) (Persian)

The Rulers
Piankhi / Shabako / Taharqa / Psamtik I / Necho / Psamtik II / Amasis / Psamtik III / Cambyses / Darius I / Xerxes / Nectanebo II / Darius III

Civil Events
Assyrians in Egypt from 671 to 658 B.C. Rule by Kushite pharaohs. Egypt, united by the kings of Saïs after the Assyrian domination, has an economic and cultural rebirth. Trade with Greece. The construction of a canal connecting the Nile with the Red Sea is started under King Necho. Phoenician sailors, sponsored by Necho, circumnavigate Africa.

Military Events
The Kushite kings conquer the whole of Egypt and Nubia. Assyrians invade Egypt and dominate the country from 671 to 658 B.C. Psamtik, prince of Saïs, revolts and frees the country from the Assyrian domination. At Pelusium, on the Nile Delta, Psamtik III is defeated by the Persians who organize Egypt as a satrapy of their empire. Persians expelled with the aid of the Greeks; last native pharaohs; reconquest of Egypt by the Persians and conquest by Alexander the Great in 332 B.C.

Flowing 4,187 miles from its chief source at Lake Victoria, the Nile (preceding page) proceeds northward through Upper Egypt, Lower Egypt, and finally the delta, creating a long, verdant ribbon of cultivable land. Irrigation canals (above and left) have been used since predynastic times to extend available farm land. A typical valley landscape (below) bears the scars of erosion.

deciphered the Rosetta stone, estimated the unification of Egypt to have occurred in 5867 B.C., a date that has since been revised to 3200 B.C.

Even today, when Egyptologists are able to provide a comparatively detailed portrait of Nilotic civilization, there are many who cling to the intriguing but mistaken notion that the ancient Egyptians were a strange and morbid people. We have abundant evidence that the ancient Egyptians enjoyed the good things in life, from fine wines to exquisite jewelry and exotic perfumes. Yet no matter how many times we are told that their culture was neither humorless nor death obsessed, it is understandably difficult to comprehend what would motivate so many individuals to set aside their finest possessions for use in the tomb. The profoundly conservative temperament of the Egyptians may be alien to us, but we tend to forget that modern technological society, engaged in a ceaseless struggle to conquer nature, would no doubt have seemed equally morbid to the ancient Nile dweller.

In fact, ancient Egypt seems gentle and optimistic when ranked with history's other great empires. Civil order was based on religious faith rather than on draconian law codes and punishments. Pharaohs boasted of their conquests, but gratuitous slaughter and cruelty were the exception rather than the rule. And if

Above, the craggy face of Upper Egypt. In some places, the habitable river valley is less than two miles wide. Despite extensive irrigation, Egyptian peasants have almost always lived and worked within sight of the desert.

the status of women can be taken as one measure of a society's development, as some historians have claimed, then the Egyptian civilization was ahead of its contemporaries—more advanced, in fact, than some modern nations.

Herodotus, the fifth-century B.C. historian who was wrong about so many aspects of Egyptian society, was at least half right when he called Egypt the "gift of the Nile." The river was benevolent, to be sure, but it was also a taskmaster that forced the civilization of the valley dwellers into well-defined and inflexible patterns. Compared with the fertile alluvial plains of the Tigris-Euphrates or the Indus, the valley of the Nile was narrow and inhospitable. For most of the 750-mile stretch between the First Cataract at Aswan and the Mediterranean Sea, the valley was merely a green ribbon no more than fourteen miles, and sometimes as little as two miles, in width. Even the rich

The fortunes
of the Nile

The fortunes of the ancient Nile dwellers were tied to the river's inexorable three-season cycle: Inundation, Emergence of the Fields, and Harvest. The world's first workable solar calendar—twelve months of thirty days each, with five extra days at the end of the year—arose out of the need to predict the arrival of these all-important seasons. In later times, stone markers were erected near Cairo and at the First Cataract to measure the Nile's flow.

The life of the peasants who maintained the valley's extensive system of irrigation ditches, catch basins, and dikes has hardly changed since ancient times, and some primitive tools, such as the weighted bucket known as the *shaduf,* are still in use today. The peasants toiled unceasingly. Even during Inundation, when the fields lay idle, peasant workers were frequently called on to perform unpaid communal labor, either on public works or on royal monuments. Nevertheless, the Egyptians accepted their dependence on the river as the norm, and countries with adequate rainfall were said to have a "Nile in the sky."

Above, Hapy, the plump blue god of the Nile's inundation, as he appears in a painting from the tomb of Queen Nefertari. This minor divinity was represented as androgynous, with a man's face and pendulous female breasts that signify abundance.

The Nile was Egypt's only highway. River boats equipped with sails appeared as early as 3100 B.C. The shallow craft steered by a stern oar (right), from the Eighteenth Dynasty tomb of Sen-nefer, is not unlike the triangular-sailed feluccas of today. Below left, a more substantial Nile boat, depicted in a mosaic of Roman times.

The Nile in full flood (below right) is a rare sight now that modern dams and flood-control projects have altered its once invariable rhythms.

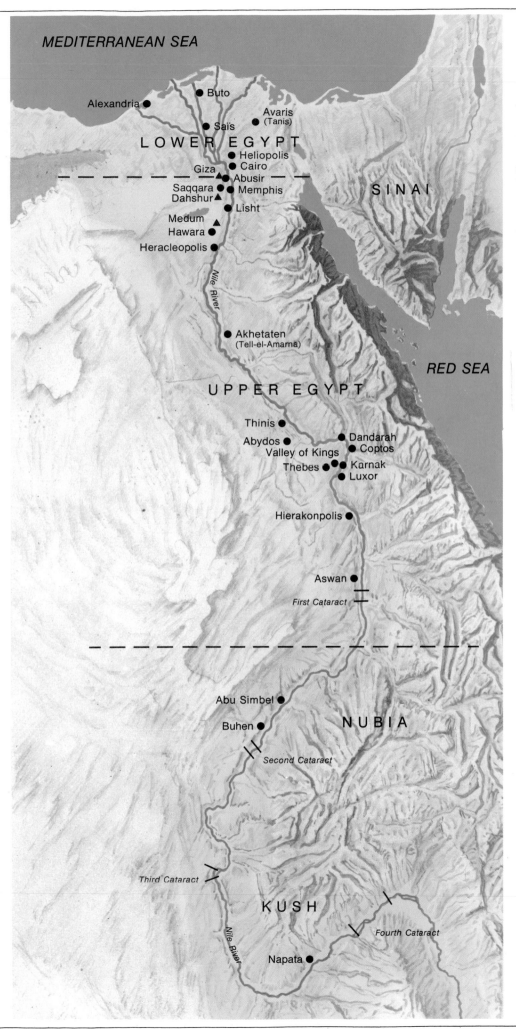

MEDITERRANEAN SEA

Buto

Alexandria

Avaris
(Tanis)

Saïs

LOWER EGYPT

Heliopolis

Giza
Cairo

Abusir

Saqqara
Memphis

Dahshur

Lisht

Medum

Hawara

Heracleopolis

Nile River

SINAI

Akhetaten
(Tell-el-Amarna)

RED SEA

UPPER EGYPT

Thinis

Dandarah

Abydos
Coptos

Valley of Kings

Thebes
Karnak

Luxor

Hierakonpolis

Aswan

First Cataract

Abu Simbel

Buhen

NUBIA

Second Cataract

Third Cataract

KUSH

Fourth Cataract

Nile River

Napata

Because the Nile flows northward, the delta region (above) came to be known as Lower Egypt, while the valley to the south was called Upper Egypt. The region south of the First Cataract (bottom) is now called Nubia. Among the ancient kingdoms of the desert was Kush, which extended south of the Second Cataract (immediately below).

The power of the written word

Renaissance astrologers and metaphysicians were convinced that hieroglyphs were esoteric symbols containing the key to a long-lost mystic rite or philosophical system. Even Jean-François Champollion, the French linguist who worked for fourteen years before deciphering a single word of hieroglyphic writing, only reluctantly abandoned the belief that each individual picture must represent a separate object or idea.

Hieroglyphs can be either pictograms or phonograms. The Egyptians used twenty-four signs portraying single consonants in addition to a repertoire of signs that stood for two or three consonants together. Since vowel sounds were not represented and the same group of consonants could suggest more than one word, pictorial signs were added to serve as determinants, giving a visual clue to the proper context.

An art form as well as a means of communication, hieroglyphic inscriptions proved cumbersome for everyday use. Instead of abandoning the system in favor of a true alphabet, the Egyptians developed a simplified script, known as hieratic, written with a pen on papyrus. Much later, in the seventh century B.C., a still more simplified form called demotic came into being.

Left, the Rosetta stone, named for the town in the delta where it was found by an engineer in Napoleon's army in 1799. This famed basalt tablet records a state decree written in 196 B.C. during the reign of Ptolemy V. Its parallel inscriptions in hieroglyphs (top), demotic (middle), and Greek (bottom) proved to be the key to deciphering Egyptian writing.

The Palermo stone (below) is a fragment from a black basalt tablet containing a list of kings from the First through the Fifth dynasties. Now preserved in the Sicilian city for which it is named, it is one of six existing fragments that probably stood in Egyptian temples.

Below, an example of hieratic script from the time of Rameses V (1152–1148 B.C.). Hieratic script became the writing of commonplace documents, while the more time-consuming, but more beautiful, hieroglyphic writing was retained primarily for paintings and stone inscriptions.

This statuette of a scribe named Kay (left) dates from about 2470 B.C. Since Egypt never developed a currency, accounts kept by scribes were crucial for recording transactions in labor and goods. The office of scribe was a privileged position—all scribes were exempt from taxes.

Stalks of the papyrus plant (right), woven together in thin slices and then beaten to form a smooth sheet, made a durable writing material.

A badly damaged papyrus from the Museo del Castello in Milan (above) and a remarkably well-preserved funerary papyrus (below), now in the Louvre, contain excellent examples of Egyptian handwritten scripts. Hieratic writing changed dramatically over the centuries, becoming less pictorial and more cursive.

Right, a hieroglyphic inscription from the Twentieth Dynasty tomb of Rameses VI.

By the time Upper and Lower Egypt were unified under a single ruler in about 3200 B.C., the Nile Valley had already been inhabited for at least two thousand years. Sir Flinders Petrie, the first archaeologist to apply scientific principles to the study of predynastic Egypt, also began the work of excavating and dating artifacts of these Neolithic cultures, whose complex history reflects a gradual progress toward organized agricultural communities. Distinctive predynastic artifacts include the flint knife (left), whose carved ivory handle depicts a battle in progress; a slender black-topped vase (immediately below); and a decorated vase (bottom) from the Neolithic Gerzean culture.

land of the delta posed problems for would-be farmers. This fan-shaped area was much marshier than it is today and was crossed by seven separate river mouths and innumerable small channels.

The essence of the Nile's gift was not unlimited abundance but the regularity of its flood cycle. Every spring, torrential rains and melting snows from the Ethiopian highlands swelled the channel of the Blue Nile, one of the river's parent tributaries. By June, the flood waters reached Aswan, and by August, they covered the entire valley as far north as the delta. The Inundation reached its peak in September and October and then began to recede, signaling the start of the season known as the Emergence of the Fields.

The first people to farm the fertile black soil deposited by the Nile had been driven to the river's edge by a long-term climatic shift that transformed what was once rolling grassland into hostile desert. Ignorant of the river's geography, they regarded the annual flood as a miracle. According to legend, the waters sprang from secret caverns in the region of Aswan. Even these early farmers, however, could not help noticing that the flood was a predictable miracle. There were, of course, lean years when the waters did not rise high enough to soak all the land under cultivation, just as there were years when an abnormally high flow washed out whole villages.

Despite these variations, the dates of high and low water remained fixed, as they did until the advent of modern flood-control techniques. A pattern of local communal agriculture was established as early as the fourth millennium B.C., when farmers learned to tame the flood by building irrigation ditches, catch basins, and dikes. In fact, one of the earliest titles bestowed on local chieftains was "Canal Builder." A ceremonial mace head now in the Ashmolean Museum shows Scorpion, a ruler of the southern river valley, presiding over a ceremonial opening of the dikes, much as a modern ruler would officiate at a ribbon cutting.

Egypt was never completely isolated. Even during this so-called predynastic period, there were undoubtedly contacts with Near Eastern peoples, and some scholars theorize that the inception of Egyptian civilization followed an invasion of the Nile Delta by Semitic tribes. The record of this period is both complicated and controversial, yet it is clear that the Egyptians borrowed only those foreign ideas that suited their peculiar environment. The idea of writing, for example, probably came from the Sumerians, but Egyptian script was unique, as was the use of papyrus as a writing material. The wheel, on the other hand, was not vital in a country where the river

The falcon god Horus (below) appears once again as a symbol of kingship in this First Dynasty stele identifying King Djet. Horus is represented atop a serekh, an abstract representation of the royal palace; the serpent within is a hieroglyph for the king's name.

The conquest of Lower Egypt by Narmer, a ruler of the south, is commemorated in this slate votive palette. Narmer (above left) wears the tall, conical crown of Upper Egypt as he prepares to strike a captive. The king's false beard and tail are symbols of his royal powers. In honor of the sacred occasion, he has removed his shoes. An attentive sandal-bearer waits to his left. The falcon to the king's right, representing Narmer, stands victorious over a human-headed form, from which six stalks of papyrus—indigenous to the delta—are sprouting in profusion.

On the obverse side of the palette (above right), Narmer is wearing the tufted crown of the newly conquered land of Lower Egypt, as he and a procession of his priests and standard-bearers inspect rows of decapitated soldiers. Beneath this grim scene, two fanciful beasts, or serpopards, are depicted with intertwined necks, symbolizing the unity of the Two Lands. The circular depression was for mixing cosmetics.

was used for transportation. Perhaps most important, the earliest Egyptians did not follow the pattern of their Near Eastern contemporaries in becoming urbanites. Though they lived in towns and cities, these settlements were seldom surrounded by walls, and all lacked compact civic centers. This failure to develop strong civic loyalties actually pushed the Egyptians in the direction of national unity.

If the Nile Valley was a natural political unit, it was also an ever-present symbol of self-renewal. Early in Egyptian history, this truth was expressed in the person of a god-king who provided a link between temporal power and spiritual authority—and be-

tween the realms of the living and the dead. Osiris, the mythical first king of Egypt, was both a fertility god and a teacher of the civilized arts. Slain by his jealous brother Seth, who locked the god's body inside a trunk and flung it into the Nile, Osiris was still able to revive sufficiently to sire a son and heir, Horus. Later, after receiving proper burial at the hands of his loyal wife, Isis, Osiris became the ruler of the Land of the Westerners—the traditional realm of the dead—while his son assumed the role of king on earth.

Despite the metaphorical logic of the Osiris legend, the unifier of Egypt was not a teacher but a con-

Right, a seated figure of Imhotep, the first nonpharaoh to be mentioned by name in Egyptian history. Imhotep was the architect of the Step Pyramid and vizier of the kingdom during Djoser's reign. He is also credited by legend with being the father of medical science.

queror. Tradition holds that the name of the first pharaoh was Menes. (Technically, the term "pharaoh" is an anachronism in this context. The title, meaning "Great House," did not come into use until the New Kingdom.) Egyptologists prefer to identify this shadowy figure as Narmer, the name of the king glorified on a famous ceremonial palette that is the earliest record of the conquest of the delta kingdom of Lower Egypt by the southern kingdom of Upper Egypt—so named because the Nile flows from south to north. The unification of these two realms into a single entity known as the Two Lands occurred in about 3200 B.C., but Upper and Lower Egypt

Flanked by two goddesses (right), the pharaoh Menkaure reflects the self-assurance of the Fourth Dynasty, when the institution of divine kingship was at its height. Below, Khafre, another Fourth Dynasty king. Here he is represented in a traditional ceremonial pose and (facing page) in the world-famous Sphinx at Giza. Above, the Sphinx of Memphis, a much later example dating from the Eighteenth Dynasty.

never lost their distinct identities. Twice more, with a predictability that gives credence to the idea that history is cyclic, periods of national turmoil were resolved by a conqueror who came out of the bleak, cliff-rimmed valley of the south to establish hegemony over the prosperous delta.

Narmer, or one of his immediate successors, established a capital at Memphis, just south of the delta. Little is known of the first two dynastic families to rule there, but the Third Dynasty produced a noteworthy king named Djoser, who set the pattern for pharaonic leadership. Djoser extended Egypt's southern boundary to the First Cataract of the Nile at

Following page, the great pyramids of Giza. The lone survivors of the fabled Seven Wonders of the Ancient World, these monuments have fascinated visitors since Greek and Roman times.

Aswan and opened the eastern desert to gold mining. Above all, he was the first pharaoh to build himself a monumental stone tomb, which dramatized his special status as a god on earth.

Oddly enough, though the form of the pyramid symbolized the exalted rank of the pharaoh over the indistinguishable masses, we know the name of the individual who invented the form. The Step Pyramid

that Imhotep, the first of a long line of vizier-architects in Egyptian history, created for Djoser was simple in design—nothing more than six *mastabas,* or flat-topped tombs, rising in stepped stages. In practice, however, the construction of the world's first monumental stone building was a daring achievement. Fashioned out of stone blocks cut to the approximate size of clay bricks, the pyramid complex included underground chambers, exquisitely decorated exterior chapels simulating the buildings Djoser had frequented in his life, and a system of internal buttressing designed to keep the enormously heavy structure from collapsing.

The art of pyramid building reached its height under the Fourth Dynasty, as did the power of the god-king to shape his subjects' lives both on earth and in the next world. Fourth Dynasty rulers made a practice of keeping important offices within the royal family. Their authority was also based on the expectation that they would continue to rule in the next world as Osiris. The right to build a private tomb was a privilege granted solely by the crown. At the royal necropolis at Giza, for example, the mastabas of princes, princesses, and nobles were huddled in the shadows of the great pyramids of Khufu, Khafre, and Menkaure.

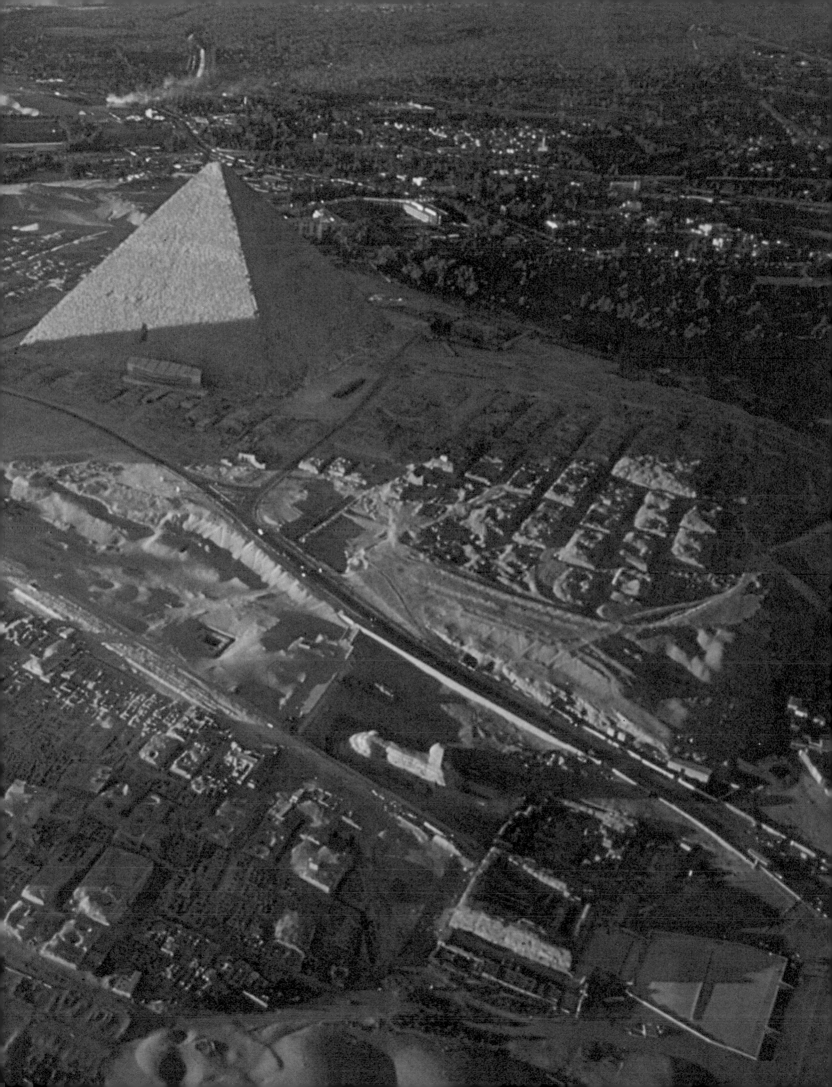

Bread and beer

"Behold I have heard that there is grain in Egypt; go down and buy grain there, that we may live. . . ." This charge by the patriarch Jacob to his sons reflects Egypt's reputation as a land capable of producing surplus grain to tide its people through times of famine. Life for the peasantry was hard, but compared to their neighbors, Egyptians ate well. Bread and beer—the latter produced from fermented, half-baked loaves—were the staples of the poor. The upper classes consumed prodigious quantities of beef and waterfowl, in addition to fruits and fancy cakes. Fish from the Nile, however, were considered unclean. In fact, both seafood and pork were forbidden to royalty and priests.

The rudimentary wooden plow (left) had to be driven into the soil by a stooping peasant. Harvest in the mythical Fields of Yalu (below) was comparatively pleasant work. This painting from the tomb of a craftsman named Senedjem reflects the belief that the deceased might be asked to perform labor in the domains of Osiris.

Viticulture (top left) was a specialty of the northeastern delta. The wealthy were connoisseurs, savoring vintage wines of at least six different varieties. Jugs found in Akhenaten's palace bore labels distinguishing between "good wine," "very good wine," and "very, very good wine."

Right, scenes of country life from a polychrome relief found in an Old Kingdom tomb at Saqqara. Immediately below, the winnowing of grain to separate kernels from chaff. Center right, a peasant tending cattle.

Once grain was harvested, maidservants (above) ground it by hand on flat stones. The model of a granary (right) shows a scribe keeping records of production. Since taxes were normally paid in goods, the scribe was in an ideal position to receive graft, and there are indications that some dishonest scribes became quite wealthy.

The common man

According to Herodotus, Egyptians were in the habit of interrupting their dinner parties to display model coffins to their guests. The Egyptian belief that one should contemplate death while still in the prime of life has contributed to the misconception that the Egyptians were a relentlessly grim people. There is considerable evidence, however, that the Nile dwellers were fun loving and optimistic. Scores of tomb paintings feature scenes of convivial banquets, family hunting parties, and camaraderie among workers. Surviving love poems record passionate attachments between men and women: "When I kiss her," said one suitor, "then I am happy even without beer." By our standards, there was little concern for the aspirations of the peasant masses, but everyone could partake equally of the land's bounty. As one New Kingdom writer boasted: "Here the humble man is like the great elsewhere."

Right, an affectionate couple, Reherka and his wife, Meresankh. Below, an unusually expressive portrait of a priest from the Twenty-fifth Dynasty. This is a late development of the so-called block statue, popular since Middle Kingdom times.

The twenty-nine-inch-high statue of the scribe Petamenopet (right) from Karnak is one of many representations of scribes at work. The training in scribal schools was arduous. Though the jobs of most scribes were routine, the profession did offer an opportunity for boys of modest birth to escape a life of manual labor. Texts assigned to students for copying insistently stressed the desirability of the scribe's lot.

Hesire (above) holds a wand symbolizing his power as an important official under Djoser. During some periods, viziers and other administrators rose from the ranks of the common people.

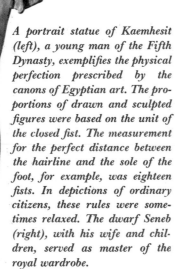

A portrait statue of Kaemhesit (left), a young man of the Fifth Dynasty, exemplifies the physical perfection prescribed by the canons of Egyptian art. The proportions of drawn and sculpted figures were based on the unit of the closed fist. The measurement for the perfect distance between the hairline and the sole of the foot, for example, was eighteen fists. In depictions of ordinary citizens, these rules were sometimes relaxed. The dwarf Seneb (right), with his wife and children, served as master of the royal wardrobe.

33

Scholars searching for words to describe the Old Kingdom, which encompassed the Third through Sixth dynasties, have used terms such as "totalitarian" and "collectivist." Certainly the very existence of the pyramids testifies to a high degree of centralization. Much of the labor was skilled, and the very logistics of quarrying the stones and moving them to the building site must have required sophisticated organization. Quarrying tools were limited to copper chisels, stone hammers, and possibly abrasive drilling powders such as quartz and pumice. Limestone, the basic building material, was available nearby, but granite, also used in substantial quantities, was quarried at Aswan and brought down river by boat.

Any attempt to characterize the spirit in which this monumental labor was accomplished is doomed to end in speculation. Herodotus was convinced that the pyramids were built at the whim of despots, constructed by armies of slaves toiling under the lash. This view was apparently supported by the Egyptian priests of his day, for they regaled him with stories about the tyrannies of Khufu, or Cheops, as he was known in Greek. These tales, already two thousand years old when Herodotus heard them, contradict a preponderance of evidence that the laborers were reasonably well treated. Some modern writers have even suggested that the construction of the pyramids served as a public works project, keeping peasants busy and well fed during the Inundation season, when the fields lay idle. And other historians have argued that the pyramids, though dedicated to a single ruler, expressed the religious fervor of an entire people.

Speculation aside, we know for certain that the culture of the Old Kingdom would be remembered in later times as having achieved the classic expression of the ideals of beauty and order. We also know that this exemplary stability did not endure. As early as the Fifth Dynasty, pyramids were becoming less ambitious, degenerating from the solid stone structures of the Fourth Dynasty into stone-covered piles of brick and rubble. Pharaohs devoted more of their resources to building temples to Re, the sun god, who by now shared power with Osiris as ruler of the dead. Above all, the nobility was no longer content to live and die in the shadow of the pharaoh's divine glory. Private tombs gradually grew more elaborate, and some even were constructed far from the royal necropolis, in the home provinces of the deceased.

Pepi II, the last ruler of the Sixth Dynasty, faced these disturbing tendencies when he came to the Throne of Horus as a young boy. He ruled for ninety years, the longest reign in recorded history, and came about as close as any pharaoh ever came to achieving

A detail from the limestone reliefs in the tomb of the Fifth Dynasty nobleman Ty at Saqqara (above left) shows a peasant leading an ox to slaughter. Left, a group of sculptors at work in their shop. Artists were not expected to be self-expressive. Instead, their work was intended to reflect the eternal verity of the spirit of ma'at. Right, two wooden statuettes of common people from Fifth Dynasty tombs: a hunchback (near right) from the mastaba of Mitri at Saqqara and a man wrapped in a cloak (far right) from the pyramids at Abu-sir (top right). Hunchback figurines, often bearing large phalluses, made popular talismans.

During the Old Kingdom, a number of large necropolises grew up in the vicinity of Memphis. In addition to Giza, site of the great Fourth Dynasty pyramids, there was Abu-sir (top), where Fifth Dynasty kings built both pyramids and temples dedicated to the sun god Re. The entrance to the inner chambers of the tomb of Mereruka (immediately above), a vizier of the early Sixth Dynasty, exemplifies a trend toward more elaborate private burials.

immortality on this side of the tomb. When the aged king finally died, the Old Kingdom collapsed precipitously, and Egypt entered a dark age known to us by the colorless name of the First Intermediate Period. No one is certain what caused this slide into anarchy. One theory holds that it may have been touched off by a series of natural disasters and the breakdown of the all-important irrigation system.

The decline of pharaonic power threw Egypt into a mood of despair. Narratives describing the period tell of mass suicides and lament that "the poor of the land have become rich; the possessor of property is now one who has naught." Such accounts were written long after the fact, and the skeptic may be excused for wondering whether the state of affairs they describe was entirely unwelcome—at least from the point of view of those who were becoming rich. But since agricultural prosperity depended on the smooth functioning of collectively maintained dikes and canals, it is easy to believe that the breakdown of order injured the common man, however much it may have benefited ambitious local families.

The uncertainties of the age had an unsettling effect on many established beliefs. Some people turned to hedonism, and one of the best-known texts of the period, the Song of the Harper, warns cynically: "Have a good time . . . it is not given to man to take

his property with him." Of course, the deep-rooted Egyptian belief in life after death would not die so easily, though some lasting changes in Egyptian funeral customs can be traced to this era. For the first time, individual Egyptians began to worry about their personal relationship to *ma'at*, hitherto a passive principle of order that was perceived to underlie the workings of the universe. This preoccupation marked the beginning of a new awareness that the great Egyptologist J. H. Breasted termed the "dawn of conscience."

Like so many ringing phrases, the "dawn of conscience" is susceptible to misinterpretation. Egyptians of this era were far from giving up their faith in ritual or becoming democrats, but they did express a new

Below left, Mentuhotep II, who reunified the Two Lands after the chaos of the First Intermediate Period, wearing the crown of Lower Egypt. In a further gesture of reconciliation, Sesostris I (below right) receives the embrace of Ptah, god of Memphis. Thebes, the home city of both of these Middle Kingdom rulers, began its rise to national prominence at this time, around 2000 B.C. Facing page, the ruins of the Ramesseum, one of several great monuments in the vicinity of the city.

consciousness of themselves as individuals. One interesting consequence was that the realm of the dead became a good deal less exclusive. The concept of a last judgment by the gods, the Weighing of the Heart, originally applied only to the pharaoh and his family, but it was now broadened to encompass the nobility. Under the New Kingdom, the judgment for the afterlife would be extended still further to include commoners; eventually, the Journey to the West was within the reach of anyone who could afford a proper burial, and the title Osiris was indiscriminately awarded to any Egyptian after death.

The rulers of the First Intermediate Period may have aspired to be as godlike as their Old Kingdom

At the Weighing of the Heart (above), the deceased was tested in the balance against a feather, representing ma'at, *or truth. The jackal-headed god, Anubis, does the weighing, while the ibis-headed Thoth, god of wisdom, stands by to record the results. The scene is from one version of the Book of the Dead.*

Under the Middle Kingdom, vessels might be 150 feet long with crews of up to 120 sailors. This ancient model (below) shows the double oar at the stern, which Egyptian pilots used in lieu of a rudder.

predecessors, but in reality, they were little more than feudal princes striving to maintain a semblance of authority over their fellow nobles. After a long period of inconclusive skirmishes among local rivals, the Two Lands were finally reunited under Mentuhotep II around 2040 B.C., marking the beginning of the Middle Kingdom. When his last direct descendant died in about 1991 B.C., the office of pharaoh was passed on to a commoner, the vizier Amenemmes. It was Amenemmes who founded the Twelfth Dynasty and carried on the work of restoring Egypt to its former grandeur.

One senses that the pharaohs of the Twelfth Dynasty were great strivers, driven by their need to assert their supremacy over the hereditary local nobilities. Amenemmes himself was the victim of an attempted coup, and in an instruction addressed to his son, he warns darkly that "a king must look after himself." His descendants heeded this advice, but even as they expanded their authority, they recognized their duties to their subjects. In portraits of this era, facial expressions suggestive of weighty responsibilities replace the serene countenances of the Old Kingdom.

Both culturally and politically, the Middle Kingdom laid the basis for the rise of the Egyptian Empire. Sesostris III fortified the Nile as far south as the Second Cataract and brought this northern sector of Nubia firmly under Egyptian control. There was trade with Punt to the south, with Crete, and with Lebanon and Syria, where Egyptian influence was reinforced by a punitive military expedition. At home, literary expression flourished, and rock-cut tombs, less of a temptation to robbers, gradually replaced the more impressive mastabas.

Middle Kingdom pharaohs paid as much attention to public works as to their tombs. Old canals and irrigation systems were repaired, and the marshy depression of the Fayum, south of the delta, was re-

A prince named Amen-her-kopshef (above) is captured for eternity in the act of burning pellets of incense. In traditional Egyptian art time stood still, and kings like Sobekhotep III (left) were forever young.

Semitic prisoners with their arms bound are portrayed (right) with remarkable realism on this stele, now in the Cairo Museum. Each prisoner personifies a conquered city-state, identified by the inscription in front of him. The Amu, or Asiatics, were heartily despised for their barbarian customs, but they proved to be Egypt's most formidable rivals.

The army in parade and action

When the Nineteenth Dynasty scribes set down the official narratives of Rameses the Great's encounter with the Hittites at the battle of Kadesh, they gave the pharaoh credit for having slain thousands of the enemy. In truth, pharaohs of this period commanded a professional army, organized into divisions of five thousand men each, with a separate supply corps and elite companies of charioteers. During the Nineteenth Dynasty, copper arrowheads and two-piece tempered bows replaced the crude archery equipment of earlier times, and soldiers of higher rank adopted the practice of wearing body armor. Rameses' leadership was, if anything, the weak point in the Egyptian military machine. Even his nation's own official account of the struggle suggests that Rameses' notions of strategy were naive compared with those of his enemies.

The horse and the war chariot (above) were introduced into Egypt by the Hyksos. Chariots were pulled by a pair of horses and occupied by two men—an archer and a driver.

A fierce naval scene is recalled on this relief (below) from Saqqara. Egypt never had a separate navy, but during the New Kingdom the army possessed warships carrying up to 250 soldiers.

Above, a bronze axe, dagger, and spearheads. Model soldiers from the tomb of a Middle Kingdom noble vividly recall a more primitive era of warfare. Above right, an infantry company. Nubian bowmen (below) were recruited as early as the reign of the Sixth Dynasty King Pepi I. They used bows with a single curve.

claimed. It was also in the Fayum that Amenemmes III built next to his pyramid a funerary temple fabled throughout classical times as the prototype of the Labyrinth of Knossos. Unfortunately, time has not been kind to the monuments of the Middle Period; of this once celebrated structure nothing survives. One Twelfth Dynasty monument, however, had a symbolic importance that far surpassed its modest size. This was the shrine to Amon begun at Karnak near Thebes by Sesostris I. Amon, whose name means "hidden," was a local Theban divinity of unknown origins. Under the New Kingdom, his renown was so well established that his followers transformed his shrine at Karnak into an immense temple-palace. Amon eventually became the patron of conquerors, and his name came to enjoy an international reputation that, centuries later, would impress Alexander the Great.

For all its energy, the Middle Kingdom collapsed in about 1790 B.C., and Egypt was again plunged into confusion—the Second Intermediate Period. This disintegration has traditionally been blamed on the Hyksos, a race of shepherd-kings. These barbarians supposedly swept into the Nile Valley from Asia, conquering all before them by dint of their ruthlessness and superior weaponry. It now appears that this standard portrait of the Hyksos was highly colored by Egyptian chauvinism. Archaeological records from the delta region are sketchy, but it seems that an Asiatic people gradually became established there under the Middle Kingdom. The Hyksos, whoever they were (the name means nothing more than "foreign chieftains"), were undoubtedly good soldiers, but it is also highly likely that they benefited from the discontent of delta nobles, who resented the centralizing policies of the Twelfth Dynasty. In a strict sense, there may have been no invasion at all.

The Hyksos established their capital at Avaris in the delta, where they adopted at least the outward forms of Egyptian culture—including the worship of

The glorious Eighteenth Dynasty made Thebes its capital and elevated the Theban god Amon to a deity of international renown. The prominent role played by the women of this family is epitomized by Hatshepsut, who assumed male titles and prerogatives and built for herself the dramatically situated mortuary temple at Deir-el-Bahri (following page). Hatshepsut's actual tomb, never completed, lay behind the high cliffs in the Valley of Kings.

Above, a statue usually identified as Amenhotep I, second king of the Eighteenth Dynasty. It stands before the eighth pylon of the Temple of Amon at Karnak.

Left, Hatshepsut's parents, Thutmose I and his "divine wife" Ahmose, depicted at Deir-el-Bahri. A chapel of the temple (above right) is dedicated to Anubis, god of cemeteries and embalming.

This representation of the queen of Punt (right) amply demonstrates that the rule of portraying important people as perfect physical specimens did not apply to foreigners. A successful expedition to Punt in East Africa was one of the high points of Hatshepsut's reign.

the ambiguous god Seth. Some historians have even speculated that the pharaoh served by Joseph in the Bible was actually a Hyksos king. But if the Hyksos managed to pass themselves off as legitimate rulers in the north of the country, they never had the same success in Upper Egypt. Thebes remained a center of rebellion.

Considering the Egyptians' low opinion of Asiatic culture, the experience of foreign rule must have been humiliating and the battles of liberation bitter. Visitors to the Cairo Museum are still shown the mummy of one Seventeenth Dynasty Theban, Seqenenre the Brave, who is said to have been killed by a blow to the head in one such engagement. For all their patriotism, the Thebans finally triumphed only after they had adopted some of the ways of their despised enemies. By the time the last of the Hyksos rulers was crushed, Egyptian armies were also fighting with horse-drawn chariots and bronze weapons.

Change did not come easily to Egypt, but the effort of expelling the Hyksos set the country on a course from which there was no turning back. The assumption of the throne of the Two Lands by Seqenenre's nephew Ahmose in about 1570 B.C. marked the be-

ginning of the New Kingdom and of Egypt's five-hundred-year-long imperial age. Egypt had never been a land of great military traditions, but once the army had been built up, it could be used abroad as well as at home. The vigorous Eighteenth Dynasty spent much of the next two and a half centuries at war. Ahmose himself sent an army into Palestine, and his grandson Thutmose I marched all the way to the Euphrates.

At its zenith, the empire of the Eighteenth Dynasty extended from present-day Syria to the Fourth Cataract in the Sudan. Even during the height of expansionist fervor, however, the imperial ambitions of the pharaohs were limited by their subjects' reluctance to settle—and especially to be buried—beyond the familiar black soil of the Nile Valley. Egyptians were good sailors and intrepid travelers when the occasion presented itself, but the idea of living in a foreign country held little allure. Lands with normal rainfall were actually regarded as freakish—a "Nile in the sky."

Given this outlook, it is hardly surprising that the kingdom of the Nile never followed up its conquests by creating a centralized Asian empire. The periodic

Above near right, a rare portrait of a pregnant queen. The subject is Ahmose, who, according to her daughter Hatshepsut, was impregnated by Amon himself. Above far right, the pharaoh Amenhotep II, son of Egypt's greatest conqueror, Thutmose III. Amenhotep II (left) appears once again, this time as he was shown on the walls of a Deir-el-Bahri chapel, in the act of offering gifts to his "divine father" Amon.

Guarding a temple that has long since turned to dust, the Colossi of Memnon (below right) were legendary for the eerie sighing sound produced by the northernmost figure every day at sunrise. The sixty-five-foot statues actually represent Amenhotep III. The strange noise they emitted, not heard since Roman times, was probably produced by expansion of the sun-warmed stones.

Egyptian women and the sisterhood

A woman in ancient Egypt might have been a dancing girl, a temple attendant, a peasant helping her husband till the fields, a household servant with considerable responsibilities, or, under special circumstances, a ruling monarch or regent. Typically, however, she was a wife.

By the time of the New Kingdom, the wife had achieved a legal status that compared favorably with that of her nineteenth-century counterparts in England and America. She could buy, sell, and inherit property and was entitled to a portion of her husband's worldly goods. Concubines and lesser wives were found in wealthier homes, but monogamy was the rule, and the chief wife was a figure who inspired both respect and affection. "Do not supervise your wife in her house if you know that she is capable," admonishes one collection of practical wisdom. "Do not say to her, 'Where is it? Get it for us!' when she had put it in [a] useful place."

The use of the term "sister" to refer to a beloved wife has created the impression that brother-sister marriages were common. Actually, incestuous marriages were limited to the royal family. This practice suggests that the crown passed through the female line. The appearance of a single female heir, however, usually spelled the fall of a dynasty.

Hired mourners (above), tears streaming from their eyes, add their professional accompaniment to the lamentations of the deceased's family.

No banquet was complete without a contingent of dancing girls and musicians (left). Dancing girls typically wore only beads and a flimsy girdle. Harp players were often elderly men, but in this scene from the tomb of Nakht in Thebes, the instrumentalist is a woman.

This slender figurine (right) is typical of the statuettes bearing offerings that were placed in tombs to guarantee the comfort of the dead.

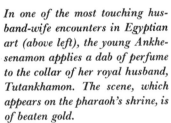

In one of the most touching husband-wife encounters in Egyptian art (above left), the young Ankhesenamon applies a dab of perfume to the collar of her royal husband, Tutankhamon. The scene, which appears on the pharaoh's shrine, is of beaten gold.

The goddess Hathor (left)—patroness of fecundity, infants, and music—appears with the pharaoh Seti I. The statuette of a nude woman (above right) is lying on a stylized representation of a funerary bed. Right, a painted limestone family group from the Fifth Dynasty.

Egyptian beauty rites

A passionate devotion to the arts of personal adornment was shared by Egyptians of both sexes. Dresses varied with the period but were usually simply styled in white linen. Jewelry, wigs, and cosmetics thus became all the more important as a means of personal expression. The eyes received the most attention, being elaborately painted with kohl, which the Egyptians mixed from ground malachite or galena. Ladies also wore rouge and stained their palms and the soles of their feet with henna.

Judging by the vast quantities of precious myrrh, unguents, and perfumed body oils the Egyptians imported, they were highly conscious of body odors and of the need to protect their skin from the dry desert climate. A lathering soap was produced from ash, and many homes contained a primitive shower, as washing in stagnant water was considered repugnant.

Hairstyles were elaborate, especially during the New Kingdom, and often included padding with artificial hair pieces. Both men and women wore wigs. In one tale, "The Story of Two Brothers," a would-be seducer is supposed to have invited his brother's wife to "put on your wig and let us spend an hour in bed."

No wealthy Egyptian lady would willingly have begun her journey to the afterlife without taking along an elaborate set of toiletries. Toilet articles (above) found in tombs include a shell for holding cosmetics, a polished metal mirror, a razor, a bone comb, and a small jar. Other cosmetic jars (left) were equipped with decorative lids as well as accessories for spreading ointments.

A son of Rameses II (left) wears the sidelock of youth, a hairstyle of preadolescent boys. Among royalty, the style may also have been the mark of a crown prince.

Right, a ceremonial wig of the New Kingdom. Wigs were composed of human hair and vegetable fibers and were sometimes ornamented with coronets, jewels, and flowers.

An attentive servant girl (above) adjusts the ear-ring of a banquet guest. The beehivelike objects on the ladies' heads are cones of scented wax. As the festivities progressed and the room grew warmer, the wax would melt, bathing their heads and shoulders in a sticky, sweet-smelling dressing.

Make-up palettes took an endless variety of forms. The prostrate female figure (below) was one distinctive type. Others were delicately carved (above right). The cylindrical container (right) was used for storing powdered make-up. Its shape recalls the segments of hollow reeds often used for the same purpose.

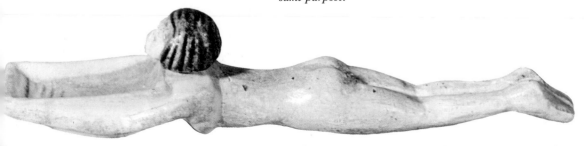

Atenism

How manifold are all thy works!
They are hidden before us.
Oh thou sole god, whose powers
no others possesseth.

On the strength of such lines from his lyrical Hymn to the Aten, the pharaoh Akhenaten (Amenhotep IV) has sometimes been hailed as the first monotheist in history. Scholars can—and do—debate endlessly the question of whether the worship of Aten was an inspired religious ideal, an egomaniacal obsession, or simply a political maneuver to break the power of

the Amonite priesthood. In any case, Aten worship was never a popular movement. Even the loyal subjects who followed the pharaoh's family to the new capital at Tell-el-Amarna were limited to approaching the god through the pharaoh and his family. Reliefs on a household shrine (above) show Akhenaten, Nefertiti, and one of their daughters (visible as a much smaller figure) adoring the solar disc whose rays terminate in small hands. The shrine itself takes the form of a massive temple pylon. The limestone statuette of Akhenaten holding an offering table (left) was also found in an Amarna villa. It depicts the pharaoh in the blue war crown.

march of an Egyptian army through Lebanon and Syria often involved little more than a show of force. After the campaign was over, the Egyptians would rule through a network of client princes. Conquered peoples might be forced to send royal hostages to Egypt and to pay tribute, but sometimes the flow of cash ran in the opposite direction. "My brother, pray send gold in very large quantities," importuned one Mitanni king in a letter to the pharaoh Amenhotep III. "Send me more gold than my father got from you. . . ."

The source of Egypt's seemingly endless wealth was Nubia. Gold had been mined in the desert east of Egypt proper since Old Kingdom times, and as the empire grew, mines were established farther south. As might be expected, this rich and immensely exploitable territory was ruled with a firm hand. The post of viceroy in Nubia was an important one, and the rulers of the Eighteenth Dynasty took up where those of the Twelfth had left off in their efforts to fortify the southern Nile and to Egyptianize this rough frontier territory. The Eighteenth Dynasty succeeded better than could possibly have been anticipated.

At home, imperialism was transforming Egyptian society. In theory, the pharaoh still ruled through his personal divinity. In practice, he stood at the head of an increasingly professional army and bureaucracy. At the bottom of the social pyramid, the ranks of the slave caste were swelled by an influx of prisoners of war. And at the top, the ruling family broke with tradition to contract marriages with foreigners. Never again would Egypt be able to turn its back on its neighbors from beyond the desert.

The Eighteenth Dynasty, which initiated and presided over these dramatic changes, was a family of energetic and strong-minded individuals. Not surprisingly, its atypical members are the ones who have captured the imagination of our time. The first of these remarkable and, to us, enigmatic rulers was

Near right, a sandstone statue of Akhenaten, one of a group discovered at Karnak. This unflattering portrait, and an even more startling companion that shows the nude pharaoh without visible genitals, seems to mock the ideal of pharaonic godliness. Later works from Tell-el-Amarna show that Akhenaten's androgynous physique—cave chested, pot bellied, and heavy thighed—had been exaggerated to the point of caricature.

Nefertiti, Akhenaten's doted-upon queen, lived up to her name, which means "the beautiful one has come." The painted limestone portrait head (below) shows the queen wearing an unusual feminine version of the pharaoh's war crown. Less well-known but even more striking is an unfinished quartzite sculpture (above) found in the studio of the royal sculptor Thutmose.

This damaged sarcophagus (above), its gold leaf stripped away in ancient times by thieves, was discovered in a remote cave in the Valley of Kings. The sarcophagus was apparently intended for a princess, but most experts agree that the bones preserved within belong to Smenkhkare, Akhenaten's ephemeral successor.

Hatshepsut. This daughter of Thutmose I was not the first woman to govern Egypt. The precedent had been set by two, possibly three, minor female rulers whose reigns signaled the demise of their dynasties. Hatshepsut, on the other hand, was technically only a regent, exercising power after the death of her young husband until the majority of his rightful heir, her stepson and nephew, Thutmose III. Even in her role as regent, Hatshepsut must have found her sex a disadvantage, for after little more than a year in power, she adopted a bold solution: She promoted herself to

king. This move went so deeply against the grain of custom that Hatshepsut was forced to have herself officially portrayed as a man. Statues show her wearing such traditional male regalia as the false beard and headdress, and she was even represented wearing a man's traditional linen skirt.

How Hatshepsut managed to hold onto the reins of power for over twenty years is a mystery. But hold on she did, erecting for herself a mortuary complex that is one of the masterpieces of Egyptian architecture, raising a pair of ninety-six-foot obelisks in her own honor at the Temple of Amon at Karnak and organizing a successful trading expedition to acquire ivory, gold, myrrh trees, and exotic spices from the fabled land of Punt in East Africa.

Supporting Hatshepsut in all these undertakings was her royal architect and personal adviser, Senmut. The suggestion is strong that Senmut was also the queen's—or rather the king's—lover. In any case, he presumed to build a tomb for himself directly under Hatshepsut's mortuary temple and to carve small images of himself in inconspicuous locations within the temple itself. Did Hatshepsut approve of his desire to be near her in death, or was Senmut scheming to collect a kind of spiritual graft? Either way, there are indications that Senmut fell from favor toward the end of Hatshepsut's reign. His temple tomb was never used, and his hidden reliefs, with the exception of a few that escaped notice, were smashed.

One enterprise in which Hatshepsut did not excel was warfare. Some Egyptologists have called her a pacifist queen, suggesting that she deliberately curtailed the expansionist policies of her predecessors. Others have gone to great lengths to prove that Hatshepsut did sponsor some campaigns. Even so, Hatshepsut's military record pales by comparison with that of her former ward, Thutmose III.

We are not certain how Thutmose gained his rightful place on the throne, but we know enough of the forceful characters of both nephew and aunt to guess that there must have been an intense rivalry between them. Possibly Thutmose found support for a coup among the priests of Amon, who may have resented the dearth of war booty, as well as Hatshepsut's claim that she had been fathered by Amon himself. Whoever the queen's enemies were, they were certainly unforgiving. After her death, they effaced Hatshepsut's name from her monuments and vengefully destroyed much of her incomparable mortuary temple.

Thutmose III, who came to power in about 1483 B.C., wasted no time in going to war. He departed on his first campaign only seventy-five days after ascending the throne, and for each of the next twenty

Left, a noble's anthropoid coffin from the Twenty-first or Twenty-second Dynasty. It is painted with gods and magic symbols, including eye amulets recalling Horus's sacrifice of an eye in his struggle with Seth.

The husband and wife in the painting (above) are playing a board game called zenet, in which the moves were determined by the casting of gaming rods.

Inherkhau (below), a Twentieth Dynasty nobleman, is surrounded by his family as he receives a votive offering from his son.

Unlucky in life, Tutankhamon achieved in death the security that eluded his more famous Eighteenth Dynasty predecessors. Its entrance hidden under a group of laborers' huts, his burial chamber (top) kept the king's mummy safe for thirty-two centuries. Tut-ankhamon's canopic shrine (left) is over six feet tall. Inside was a solid alabaster chest containing the king's vital organs.

Tutankhamon's mummy lay within three nested coffins, the third being of solid gold. The second coffin (immediately above) is gold leaf over wood. Its multicolored design of glass paste is in the rishi *pattern, mimicking the feathered wings of a goddess.*

years he made it his practice to spend at least six months in the field. In the most daring of his annual expeditions, Thutmose actually surpassed the feat of his grandfather, Thutmose I, driving deep into the territory of the Mitanni beyond the banks of the Euphrates. The Egyptian army tarried only long enough to erect a stele commemorating the occasion and to accept the surrender of the cities in the path of its homeward march. Closer to home, the pharaoh's most formidable enemy was the king of Kadesh, whose final defeat solidified Egyptian influence in Syria.

Thutmose III was a methodical military leader. Perhaps he had learned the value of careful patience under the long usurpation of Hatshepsut. His victories, the greatest of the imperial period, were largely the result of superior planning and logistics. In the obelisks he raised at home to celebrate his accomplishments, Thutmose was careful to share credit with his "father" Amon—the once obscure god who had now merged with the venerable sun god Re to become the patron deity of Egyptian expansionism.

Three of Thutmose III's four immediate successors were named Amenhotep, or "Amon-Is-Satisfied." The feeling of satisfaction must have been mutual, for these men ruled during a time of unrivaled prosperity and splendor. Amenhotep III, the warrior's great-grandson, was especially fortunate. He reigned for about forty years, devoting most of his energies to building temples and honoring his commoner queen, Tiy, who was as influential as she was beloved. Their son, the fourth Amenhotep, was another story entirely. In him, the Eighteenth Dynasty produced the unthinkable—a heretic pharaoh.

Early in this young man's reign, perhaps while he was still serving as coregent with his father, he began to worship a relatively obscure deity, the Aten, or solar disc. This devotion to a hitherto unfamiliar god might not in itself have been cataclysmic, but Akhenaten, as he was henceforth called, exhibited a most un-Egyptianlike streak of fanaticism. He tried to stamp out the old order to make way for the new.

After effacing the name of Amon from his temples, Akhenaten ordered the abandonment of Thebes and founded an entirely new capital, Akhetaten, or "Horizon-of-Aten." The city, more often known by its modern name of Tell-el-Amarna, was situated on a rather unpropitious strip of land on the east bank of the Nile halfway between Memphis and Thebes. Akhenaten chose the location because it was sacred to no other god (perhaps none had wanted it), and he set about filling the city with monuments that expressed his revolutionary concept of "living in truth." An innovative art style now replaced the majestic, timeless poses characteristic of traditional portraiture. Adopting a more naturalistic approach, artists depicted intimate, affectionate scenes of Akhenaten's domestic life with his queen, Nefertiti, and his six daughters. Here, for the first time, we see a pharaoh kissing his wife on the lips and bouncing his infant children on his lap.

But the new aesthetic revealed other features that are somewhat less appealing and more difficult to interpret. For example, in place of the rigidly idealized physiques that had previously been the rule, Akhenaten insisted that he—and, to a lesser degree, his family and followers—be portrayed with narrow shoulders, a pot belly, heavy thighs, and spindly calves. One can only assume that this new ideal reflected the pharaoh's own appearance. But why did he choose to elevate his personal peculiarities into an artistic standard? Was he motivated by a respect for realism or a desire to sweep away the hypocrisy of the past? Was he simply an egotist?

Perhaps the best-known answer to the riddle of Akhenaten was proposed by his chief defender, J. H.

A royal ostrich hunt is the fitting theme for a ceremonial fan, or flabellum (above), which originally held ostrich feather plumes. Immediately below, one of two tiny coffins that contained the remains of Tutankhamon's infant children. Bottom, a detail from the pharaoh's ornate throne representing his ceremonial name, Nebkheprure.

Breasted. In his admiration for the pharaoh's Hymn to the Aten, a song of praise that has often been compared to Psalm 104, Breasted hailed Akhenaten as the inventor of monotheism and as the "first individual in history."

For every expert who shares Breasted's admiration for Akhenaten, however, there are at least two who are prepared to advance a countertheory proposing that the heretic pharaoh was either a freak or a megalomaniac. It had been argued, variously, that Akhenaten was a mental defective, a victim of the pituitary disorder known as Froelich's Syndrome, a transvestite, and a hermaphrodite. Most of these ideas, based on literal-minded interpretations of the more bizarre Amarna portraits, contradict more substantial evidence. Another school of criticism, harder to refute, holds that Akhenaten was motivated not by ideals but by an ambition to break the power of the Amonite priests.

Certainly Akhenaten's revolution did not materialize out of thin air, and elements of the Amarna style are prefigured in works created under Amenhotep III. The ethical content of Akhenaten's beliefs is more difficult to pin down. There are intriguing hints that the pharaoh was indeed a social visionary. Villas at Tell-el-Amarna were constructed without separate women's quarters, for example, suggesting that there may have been a move toward greater equality of the sexes.

No matter what the experts may say, there will always be those who sense something peculiarly modern and sympathetic in the figure of this poet-pharaoh. We can be sure, however, that few of Akhenaten's subjects found him appealing. He insisted upon his own privileged status as a god—the only deity other than the one Aten—and tried to return his kingdom to the days when the pharaoh was the sole link between his people and the spiritual world. But a god must be surrounded by at least an aura of success, and Akhenaten was not. By the end of his brief sev-

The serene countenance of Tutankhamon's mummy mask reflects none of the turmoil and tragedy that marred the young king's life. On the mask's forehead are a vulture and a cobra, emblems of the goddesses Nekhebet and Wadjet respectively, and symbols of the united power of the Two Lands. The distinctive beard, along with the flail and shepherd's crook placed across the king's chest, indicated that a dead ruler had assumed his identity as Osiris.

Life and afterlife

One measure of the ancient Egyptian's satisfaction with his life—and of his reluctance to leave it—was his painstaking effort to make sure that the next world would mirror this one in every detail. The relatives of the deceased, or in later times the mortuary priests, were charged with providing offerings of food to sustain the *ka,* or spiritual double, of the entombed body. But such devotions were maintained for a few generations at best, and every individual recognized that the laborious task of furnishing a tomb would be primarily his own responsibility.

Naturally, maintaining a household in the afterlife would require labor. The custom of burying human attendants with their master had died out before Old Kingdom times, but in other periods, a number of ingenious solutions to the servant problem were devised. One of these was the provision of small mummiform figures known as *ushabtis* or *shawabtis,* which could be called on to perform work on behalf of the tomb's occupant. A related phenomenon was the use of tiny models who performed, in miniature, all the domestic tasks necessary to insure the comfort of the deceased. These realistic tableaux reflect with extraordinary fidelity the daily routines of ordinary men and women—people who could never have afforded to record the details of their lives in tombs of their own.

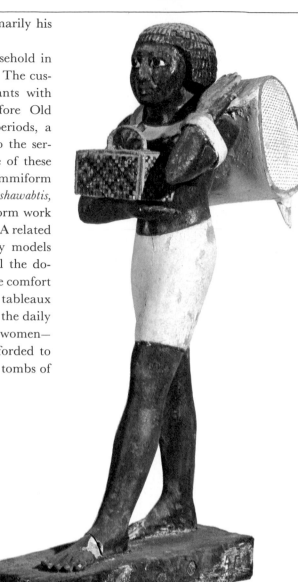

This pair of potters (left) is producing cookware and other utilitarian items. Tableware for the wealthy was commonly made of stone, metal, or glass. A cook (below left) fans the fire as he roasts skewered meat over an earthenware brazier.

Above, a Nubian porter wearing the distinctive hair style of his country. The cloth-maker's implements (below) include bronze needles as well as skeins, a bobbin, and a spindle.

In butcher shops like this one (left), cattle were slaughtered in the presence of a priest. Beef was a favorite food of the aristocracy, and Egyptians in general were prodigious meat eaters. A procession of servants (immediately below) carries food stuffs and other ritual gifts for the deceased.

Despite a chronic shortage of timber, which was often imported from Lebanon, carpenters were highly skilled and produced simple but elegant furniture. Both the carpenter's shop (bottom left) and the woman working at her loom (bottom right) are set in models of the typical Egyptian mudbrick house. Stone was used only for religious architecture, seldom for domestic buildings.

Medicinal magic

Although their practice of the healing arts never outgrew its origins in magic, Egyptian physicians enjoyed a deservedly high reputation throughout the ancient world. Many of the natural remedies they administered are now known to have been scientifically sound. Nile mud, which was often mixed into medicines, has the antibiotic Aureomycin as one of its constituents. Contraceptive jelly made of honey, dates, and powdered acacia was effective because acacia spikes contain a gum that is deadly to sperm. Surviving manuscripts show that physicians understood the value of a systematic approach to diagnosis and were especially adept at handling external wounds. Their understanding of physiology and of the causes of disease was necessarily limited, yet the Egyptians made one lasting contribution: They were the first to recognize the importance of the pulse which they called the "voice of the heart."

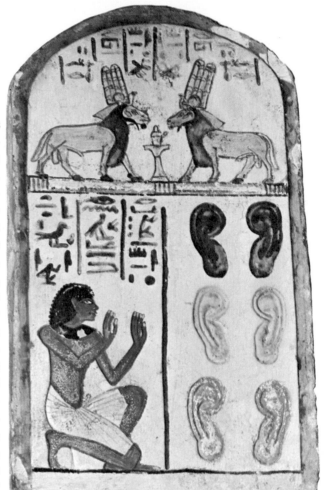

Magic and the hope of divine intercession were never completely separated from the practice of scientific medicine. This votive stele (left), dedicated to Amon-Re, stood near the door of a temple and was meant to gain a hearing from the gods.

Right, a sampling of Egyptian surgical instruments. Left, the stele of Roma, preserved in the Ny Carlsberg Glyptothek in Copenhagen. It shows a probable case of poliomyelitis.

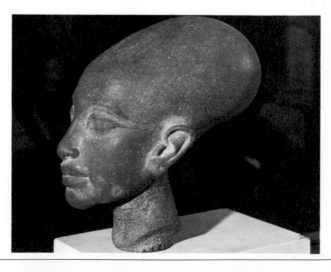

The elongated skull of this portrait head (right) representing one of the daughters of Akhenaten has inspired many modern-day diagnoses. It is most likely the product of artistic convention and was not meant to represent a pathological condition.

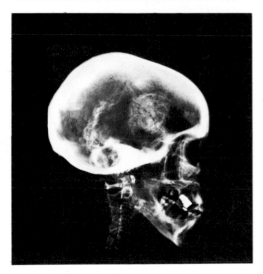

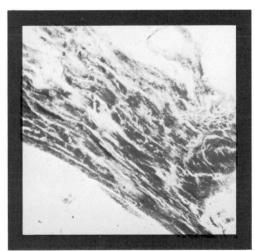

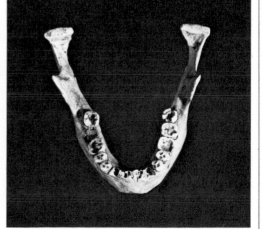

The scientific study of mummies has contributed much to our knowledge of Egyptian medicine and mummification techniques. The skull X ray (immediately above) reveals a head injury. Center right, the mummy of Rameses II, who lived to be about ninety. Center far right, tissue from a mummy, enlarged five hundred times with the aid of an electron microscope. Its structure is intact and visible after thousands of years. Bottom far right, an ancient jaw showing evidence of dental treatment.

enteen-year reign, Egypt was, as contemporary inscriptions were to say, topsy-turvy.

Even while Akhenaten remained in his new capital pursuing his experiment in a new order, the rest of his kingdom was in ferment. Egypt's foreign situation had been deteriorating since the reign of his father. A cache of clay tablets inscribed with diplomatic correspondence, discovered during excavations in a field near Tell-el-Amarna, is full of missives from distraught client priests. They warned Akhenaten of the rising power of the Hittite Empire and of the threat posed in Palestine by marauding tribes known as the Habiru—a name that tantalizes scholars because of its

similarity to "Hebrew." Whether Akhenaten could have done anything to stem this rising tide is debatable, but his influential subjects, many of whom had refused to follow him to his new capital, must have longed for some decisive action.

As long as all was well at Tell-el-Amarna, Akhenaten could presumably afford to ignore these signs of trouble from without. In the fifteenth year of his reign, however, things began to fall apart. The image and name of Queen Nefertiti, once a prominent feature of the cult of Aten, suddenly disappeared from the monuments. She was replaced by references to a young man, Smenkhkare, who was married to one of

the pharaoh's daughters and was soon to become a pharaoh himself. He may have been Akhenaten's son or brother as well. What happened to Nefertiti? One theory is that she became disillusioned with her husband and decamped. More likely, she died. Akhenaten himself soon followed her into obscurity in about 1355 B.C. His mummy, which might resolve so many questions about his apparently peculiar physique, has never been found.

The fate of Akhenaten's family is somewhat better established. In 1907, an amateur archaeologist exploring the Valley of Kings near Thebes came upon a small chamber cut into the rocks that contained the

Horemheb, the commoner who became pharaoh after the fall of the Eighteenth Dynasty, appears (far left) in his tomb in a traditional pose with the goddess Hathor. Above, a painting also from Horemheb's tomb showing four denizens of the underworld pulling the solar barge. Below, the god Atum with the "exhausted ones" looking to heaven and the "damned" en route to punishment. Following page, the ruins of the massive temple-palace of Amon-Re at Karnak.

remains of an obviously hasty burial. The partially decomposed coffin was evidently intended for a princess, but the skeleton within was that of a young man,

almost certainly Smenkhkare, who was no more than nineteen when he died. He was succeeded by his nine-year-old brother, Tutankhamon. This little boy was married to Akhenaten's daughter Ankhesenpaaten, who must have been some years older. Willingly or not, the young couple moved back to Thebes and made their peace with the priests of Amon. Like his brother, the young pharaoh Tutankhamon died while still in his late teens and was entombed along with the mummified bodies of two prematurely born female infants. Thanks to an historical accident, this pathetic dénouement to the glorious Eighteenth Dynasty has become one of the best-known episodes in all Egyptian history. While the tombs of Tutankhamon's more illustrious ancestors were being stripped of their treasures, the entrance to his burial chambers lay hidden under a group of laborers' huts erected during the construction of the tomb of Rameses VI in the twelfth century B.C. The gold of Tutankhamon, discovered by Howard Carter in 1922, was the most sensational find in archaeological history. We can only wonder how the young king's funerary treasures compared with those of his more important and long-lived ancestors.

The excavation of Tutankhamon's tomb has given the twentieth century at least some notion of the splendor and craftsmanship that prevailed during the New Kingdom. Some of the objects found inside the tomb, including the king's jewelry and domestic furnishings, may have actually been used in life. Even the more ordinary funerary provisions sometimes had great value. It was customary for tomb robbers, for instance, to concentrate on raiding the readily salable unguents and oils from newly sealed tombs. Much of the funerary treasure, however, was especially fashioned for the king's enjoyment after death. Tutankhamon's ceremonial throne does not seem sturdy enough to have seen active use, and the flotilla of model ships intended to be used by the king as he followed Re on his nightly journey was, of course, purely symbolic.

Fine as these artifacts are, some of them were obviously completed in haste. Howard Carter, for example, discovered piles of wood chips on the tomb floor left behind by careless workers. He also noted that the design of the alabaster canopic shrine, which contained the pharaoh's embalmed internal organs, did not follow the established and accepted religious pattern. Similar instances of apparent sloppiness in the face of otherwise meticulous burial preparations have been found in other tombs, but in Tutankhamon's case it does seem likely that his Overseer of Works, known to have been an individual named Maya, was forced by the pharaoh's early death to cut

Karnak's Avenue of the Rams (above left) takes its name from the distinctive ram-headed sphinxes sacred to Amon-Re that line this ceremonial approach to the first pylon. Rameses III, the empire's last truly effective pharaoh, constructed these ceremonial figures of himslf as Osiris (left). Originally a suncult monument connected with the city of Heliopolis, the obelisk made its most notable appearance at Karnak during the Eighteenth Dynasty. Hatshepsut's obelisk (above right) is ninety-six feet tall.

The Great Hypostyle Hall, completed by Seti I and his son Rameses II, is Karnak's most breathtaking monument. The bulbous capitals of its sixty-nine-foot-high columns (right) represent papyrus bundles, symbols of fertility identified with the supreme god Amon.

short preparations that would ordinarily have been more elaborate. In that case, we can only imagine that Tutankhamon's tomb contained only a fraction of the riches that were to be buried with such an important pharaoh as Amenhotep III.

In hindsight, the burial of so much gold and other wealth seems not only unfortunate but also wasteful. Yet the custom may have inadvertently served a very practical purpose. Egypt had been rich in gold since the New Kingdom. Under the empire, it was flooded with wealth from Nubia and from abroad. Without some mechanism for absorbing this bounty, the kingdom might have become quite unstable. Reserving such vast quantities of gold for the tomb helped prevent inflation and, not incidentally, the social mobility that would have resulted from the general circulation of the wealth.

As it was, wealth and authority in Egypt remained highly centralized, even during the New Kingdom. In addition to the office of the vizier, which was at this point usually divided between two individuals responsible for Upper or Lower Egypt, the pharaoh's entourage included a Supervisor of the Granaries, who directed all agricultural production and collected royal taxes on the proceeds. The bulk of Egypt's rich farm land was the ruler's personal property, and as long as it continued to produce ample food for the population, the system went unopposed.

Since women played an unusually visible role in the affairs of the Eighteenth Dynasty, it is only fitting that the last voice raised on the family's behalf should be that of a female—Ankhesenpaaten, or Ankhesenamon, as she came to be called. In a final effort to provide herself with an heir and keep the Throne of Horus in the family, this young widow wrote to the king of the Hittites, Shubilulliuma, begging him to send her one of his sons as a husband. The request was unprecedented, and the Hittite ruler delayed, sensing a trap. Once again, the widow pleaded her case in a letter: "If I had a son," she implored, "would

Seti I's rock-cut tomb in the Valley of Kings near Thebes ranks with that of Horemheb as one of the most splendid of the imperial age. The pharaoh's profile is at left. Other details from his tomb include a procession of servants (above right); Osiris, flanked by Anubis fetishes in the form of inflated animal skins (near right); and cartouches containing the royal names of the sovereign—Menmaare Seti-Merenptah (far right).

A god for any occasion

According to the cosmology of Heliopolis, the world began when the creator god Atum arose from a primeval mound and masturbated, thus becoming the sole progenitor of the first couple, Shu and Tefnut, who personified air and moisture. A more refined creation story from Memphis holds that the god Ptah willed all things into being with his heart.

The ancient Egyptians saw nothing mutually exclusive in these two myths. Their world view admitted to many truths, and their syncretistic approach to religion allowed countless gods to coexist in harmony. As local deities such as Ptah or Re, the sun god of Heliopolis, rose to national prominence, they often borrowed attributes from other gods. Amon of Thebes merged with his rival Re instead of banishing him. And the pharaohs, themselves living gods, saw nothing contradictory in identifying themselves simultaneously with Horus, Ptah, and Re. Once accepted, a god was never abandoned.

Osiris (above left), one of the oldest of Egyptian deities, was both the mythological first king of the Two Lands and the ruler of the dead. The jackal-headed god Anubis (above right) was also identified with the dead, but his function was more specific: He served as the protector of cemeteries and performed the Weighing of the Heart at the last judgment.

Horus, the falcon-headed sky god (left), was usually identified with another Horus, the son of Osiris. As such, he was the personification of earthly kingship. Pharaohs were said to occupy the Throne of Horus. Right, three other deities connected with the Osiris cycle: Isis (right), her sister Nephthys (left), and the ram-headed god Khnum (center).

Re-Harakhte, or "Horus-on-the-Horizon" (left), was a composite of two important deities, Horus and Re. In an unusual depiction, the Memphite god Ptah (right) appears with a wig and royal insignia. More often, he was shown with a shaved head. Ptah was the patron of architects, sculptors, and craftsmen. In contrast to her pacific husband Ptah, Sekhmet (below left) was the lion-headed goddess of war. She was both the instigator of epidemics and a patroness of the medical profession. The goddess Ma'at (below right) personified truth and divine order. Her symbol was the ostrich plume.

Holy animals

Gods with theriomorphic, or animallike, attributes were always plentiful in the Nile Valley. Jewelled crocodiles sacred to Sobek lolled in temple pools in the Fayum, and at Bubastis in the delta the goddess Baśtet was adored in the form of a living cat. Nevertheless, the rise of large-scale animal necropolises coincided with the dissolution of pharaonic power and a growing decadence in religious practice. During the third century B.C., a constellation of cult centers arose at Saqqara. There, in underground pits and catacombs, archaeologists have discovered thousands upon thousands of mummified baboons, bulls, ibises, and cats.

Immediately above, the mythical serpent Apophis who challenges Re every morning as the sun god begins his progress across the sky. From time to time, Apophis triumphs, producing an eclipse. The cat (left) was domesticated in Egypt by about 2100 B.C. This statuette is one of many appealing representations of the animal, which was prized for its grace as well as for its mouse-catching abilities. Baboons (right) imported from the south were also popular pets.

This image of a falcon (below) found at Deir-el-Medina was intended as a model for artists.

A bull is shown (above) in a relief from the temple of Rameses II at Abydos. The cult of Apis, the sacred bull, flourished at Saqqara, where it eventually came under the patronage of the Ptolemaic pharaohs.

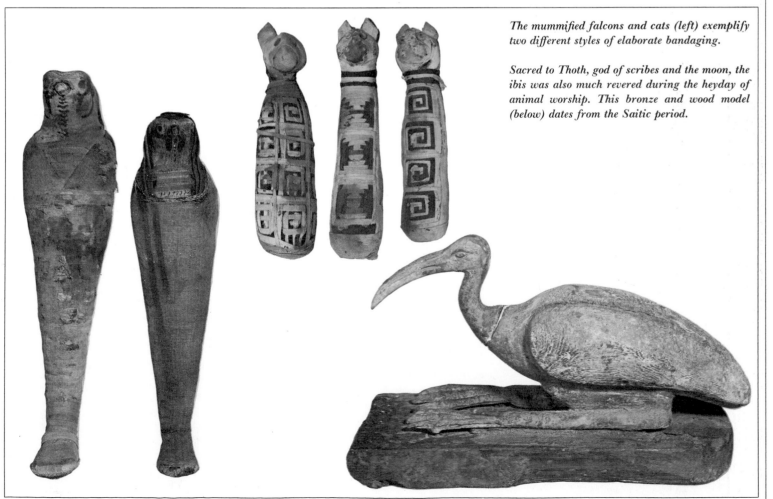

The mummified falcons and cats (left) exemplify two different styles of elaborate bandaging.

Sacred to Thoth, god of scribes and the moon, the ibis was also much revered during the heyday of animal worship. This bronze and wood model (below) dates from the Saitic period.

The names of Rameses II—
known to us as Rameses the
Great—appear (above) on his
throne over a striking symbol of
the Two Lands—a pair of Nile
gods binding the sma sign, a
hieroglyph for "unity."

Below, Rameses II holding a
trio of prisoners by the hair.
The three captives represent the
Nubians, the Libyans, and the
Asiatics. Their small size em-
phasizes their low status.

I write to a foreign country in a manner which is humiliating to me? . . . People say you have many sons. . . ." King Shubilulliuma finally saw the logic of the young woman's request. An eligible prince was dispatched, but he was murdered before he could meet and marry his Egyptian queen. No doubt there were influential people in Thebes who had had enough of the lady and her troublesome family.

Tutankhamon was succeeded by an old family retainer, Ay. This gentleman had been much maligned by writers sympathetic to Akhenaten. It was Ay who negotiated the reconciliation of Tutankhamon with the priests of Amon, and he is sometimes suspected of having schemed to marry Ankhesenamon, or worse. But if Ay can be credited with putting a halt to the plan to bring a Hittite prince to Egypt, then he was a hero from the Egyptian point of view. At any rate, Ay did not live long, and it was only after his death in 1342 B.C. that the reaction against Amarna and everything it stood for was unleashed in full force.

This basalt coronation statue (near left), over six feet high, shows Rameses II wearing a war crown and holding a crook as an insignia of command. Rameses' jewelled pectoral (above) combines three animals symbolic of royal power: the falcon, the vulture, and the uraeus, or sacred cobra.

The most dynamic era of the New Kingdom had now drawn to a close. Power passed to a series of rulers who did little more than shore up the legend of Egyptian greatness. The transitional figure between the Eighteenth and Nineteenth dynasties was Horemheb, a general who had served under Akhenaten. Even at this late stage in Egyptian history, it is difficult to characterize men by profession; the same individual may have served as a general, a royal administrator, and even a priest. Nevertheless, Horemheb fits the time-honored stereotype of the veteran soldier who is more traditionalist than royalty itself.

After restoring the confiscated property of the priesthood of Amon—even allowing the use of stones from Akhenaten's monuments in construction work on the temple complex at Karnak—Horemheb died without an heir, passing the crown to a military colleague named Rameses.

The first Rameses did not live long. His son, Seti I, waged a limited but successful battle to win back some of Egypt's lost influence in Asia. Seti's son, the second Rameses, was not so lucky. While still a young man, Rameses II led his armies in a campaign against Egypt's most powerful rival, the Hittites. The enemy forces met near Kadesh, the city that had been conquered by Thutmose III. Rameses was lured into an ambush by two Bedouins posing as Hittite deserters, and one of his divisions was massacred. The pharaoh, trapped in his camp, held off the Hittite army single-

handedly until he was joined by reinforcements. The encounter ended in an Egyptian retreat, and if we discount the obvious exaggerations in the matter of Rameses' personal valor, the battle does not seem to have been much to boast about. In fact, the long-term outcome of Rameses' campaign was the loss of the territory his father had struggled to regain.

This battle of Kadesh might not seem to be the stuff legends are made of, but Rameses calculated that whatever deficiencies he had shown as a military commander could be redressed by his skills as a propagandist. Back in Egypt, the royal scribes embroidered the story of Kadesh into a tale of epic proportions in which the pharaoh was personally responsible for the destruction of thousands of Hittite bowmen. Rameses spent the rest of his sixty-seven-year reign fathering children—some sources say he had at least

The Abu Simbel temples built by Rameses the Great are the most monumental legacy of the long Egyptian hegemony over Nubia. They have now been raised from their original site on the banks of the Nile (right) to a new location, above the waters of manmade Lake Nasser. The king's temple (left) is guarded by four, sixty-seven-foot-tall effigies of Rameses. The smaller temple (below right) honors his queen, Nefertari.

150—and raising monuments to his own glory throughout the length of the Nile Valley, from Abu Simbel in the far south to his home in the delta, where he built two great cities. Rameses II, known to history as Rameses the Great, thus succeeded in making himself Egypt's best-remembered ruler, his name virtually synonymous with pharaonic power.

Modern scholars are, for the most part, immune to Rameses' spell. Having been fortunate enough to discover contemporary Hittite accounts of the action at Kadesh, they are in a position to debunk Rameses' self-aggrandizing inscriptions. And they are also likely to be contemptuous of Rameses' great monuments, which tend to be as banal as they are enormous. In retrospect, we can see that Rameses' phenomenal building projects drew attention away from the failing health of the empire. Yet there is probably nothing that Rameses could have done to reverse this process. In the twenty-first year of his reign, he signed a nonaggression pact with the Hittites. Nevertheless, there were by now several international developments that Egypt, with its army largely dependent on mercenaries and its wealth increasingly in the hands of the Amonite priests, would be ill-prepared to meet.

Barbarian peoples, many armed with bronze or iron weapons, were on the move throughout the Mediterranean world. Rameses' son, Merenptah, already middle-aged by the time his father died in his nineties, found himself faced with a force comprised of two oddly matched allies—Libyans from the western desert and the migratory Sea Peoples from Asia Minor. Merenptah scored a seemingly decisive victory over these invaders, but when he died, his dynasty came apart completely and with this disinte-

Once a year, the image of the great god Amon left his temple at Karnak and was carried in a procession to his secondary home near the modern-day town of Luxor, south of the ancient site of Thebes. The temple at Luxor, whose first courtyard and pylon are shown at below left, was begun by Amenhotep III. Rameses the Great left his personal stamp on the site in the form of massive statuary (above left). Above right, colonnades and statues of the pharaohs in the first courtyard. Cartouches bearing the royal names of Rameses II are visible at the base of a tall obelisk (facing page). The name and image of this inveterate monument builder are ubiquitous throughout Upper Egypt. Rameses also constructed two cities in the delta, but like many other sites in Lower Egypt, they have not been thoroughly excavated.

gration came the illusion of domestic security.

His successor, Rameses III, was the founder of the Twentieth Dynasty and the progenitor of a long line of kings, all named Rameses. Like his great namesake, he was an ambitious military leader. The Libyans and the Sea Peoples continued to pose a threat to Egypt's security, so Rameses assembled his forces against them in about 1190 B.C., defeating them in two battles, including a naval encounter fought near one of the mouths of the Nile. This was the greatest naval victory in Egyptian history, and Rameses triumphantly ordered that it be commemorated in stone reliefs and inscriptions on the walls of his vast

mortuary temple, Medinet Habu, near Thebes.

Unfortunately, Rameses III resembled his renowned forebear in his passion for women as well as for building monuments. In his enthusiasm for assembling a large number of lesser wives and concubines for his household, he unwittingly set himself up for a conspiracy against his life.

Rameses' death is one of the great murder mysteries of Egyptology. Though the contemporary text describing the bizarre event is open to several different interpretations, it seems probable that one of Rameses' lesser wives, Ti, had plotted to place her own son on the throne. This was no mere whim, for

Medinet Habu (above), Rameses III's monumental mortuary temple on the west bank of the Nile, was modeled after the Ramesseum of his namesake and idol Rameses the Great. Aesthetically uninspiring, Medinet Habu has been a mecca for scholars, who search its extensive inscriptions for clues to the decline that followed the death of this Twentieth Dynasty ruler.

her allies in the conspiracy were highly placed military men, officials of the royal household, and influential members of the priesthood.

At their trial, the conspirators were accused of employing wax images of the pharaoh and his loyal followers to gain their ends. This tactic is hardly surprising, since we know that the Egyptians believed in the supernatural importance of names and images. It was traditionally believed that portrait statues, the Pyramid Texts of the Old Kingdom, and, in later times, papyrus copies of the Book of the Dead could be used to help an individual's *ka* spirit on its perilous journey to the West. The conspirators may have be-

lieved, therefore, that images formed with evil intent could also speed the living on their way out of this world.

By whatever means, the plotters brought on the death of Rameses III. The so-called Judicial Papyrus of Turin records the proceedings of a mass trial in which some of the guilty were sentenced to slavery in the mines and some mutilated. The leaders, presumably, were executed or allowed to commit suicide. (It was not characteristic of Egyptian records to gloat over such a fate. Death sentences were often described euphemistically.) The defendants were also deprived of their true names. In the record, they are referred to by curse names, signifying that the judges were as sensitive to the power of the supernatural as were the accused.

The murdered pharaoh was succeeded by his legitimate heir, Rameses IV, and, after him, by seven more Rameses—all now virtually indistinguishable. At the end of this family's rule in 1085 B.C., the unity of the Two Lands had broken down altogether, with power

*Rameses III died after the instigators of a
harem conspiracy used wax images to gain
their evil ends. The pharaoh, whose portrait
(above right) appears in his tomb, supposedly
denounced the black magic conspirators from
his grave in a famous text. Below right, two
goddesses, splendidly dressed, from a Twentieth Dynasty tomb.*

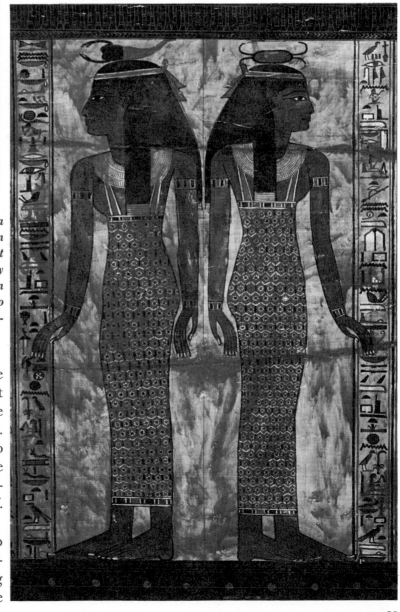

divided between a family of delta pharaohs and the
priests of Amon, who by now controlled a significant
percentage of the country's land and wealth. The
mood of these times was one of pervasive anxiety.
There are records of strikes by mortuary workers who
had not received their pay. The mines of Nubia were
no longer as productive as they once had been. Moreover, the influx of tribute from Asia had been cut off.
In short, Egypt was on the verge of bankruptcy.

As might be expected, corruption flourished. Tomb
robbing, always a problem, reached critical proportions. There is a theory that the practice of sealing
huge amounts of gold into royal tombs protected the

Funeral customs

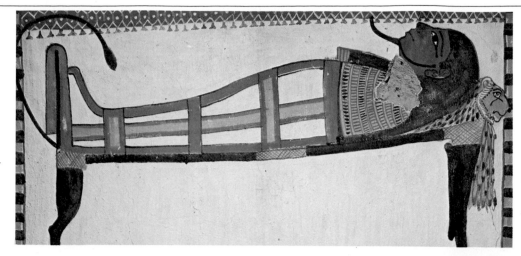

Curled in the fetal position and surrounded by a few simple possessions, Egypt's first mummies were formed in predynastic times by the natural conditions of their shallow, sandy graves. Ironically, the advent of more elaborate, more humid tombs made it necessary to dry corpses artificially by packing them in natron. Skilled embalmers removed the internal organs for separate preservation and anointed the mummy with aromatic gums, resins, and other precious substances before wrapping it up in over 400 square yards of linen. The resins and unguents often defeated their own purpose, turning the mummy into a featureless, gluey mass.

Yet the greatest enemy of the mummy was not time but the tomb robber. Some Egyptologists believe that the practice of burying massive quantities of gold in royal tombs saved the country from ruinous inflation. By the Twenty-first Dynasty, however, most of the gold had been plundered by thieves, who often tore mummies limb from limb while searching for jewelry among the linen bandages.

A mummy on its litter (top right) awaits transfer to the sarcophagus. Two scenes from the Eighteenth Dynasty tomb of Ramose (middle and bottom right) show an assembly of mourners and a funeral procession.

A portrait of the deceased (left) adorns the upper part of an anthropoid-style sarcophagus.

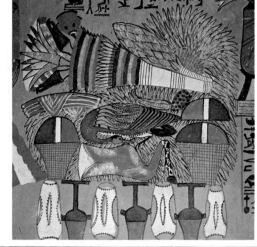

Eternal sustenance for the dead man's ka *spirit, the painted offering (right) includes artichokes, flowers, fowl, meat, and baskets of other necessary provisions.*

Above, the ceremonial preparation of the sarcophagus, in a painting from the tomb of Payri at Luxor. Near left, a detail of a painted sarcophagus decorated with symbols from the cult of the dead. Far left, an elaborately wrapped mummy now in the collection of the Egyptian Museum, Turin. The tomb of Merenptah (below), otherwise stripped bare, still contains the sarcophagus of the king.

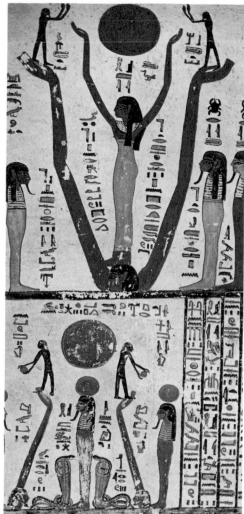

The dead man, the sun, and the sun's two boats, one for day and one for night, are represented (left) in crude magical symbols in this ceiling painting from a tomb of the Late Kingdom. Above, a painting from the tomb of Rameses VI showing a mystical image of the ka spirit with elongated upraised arms supporting a goddess on its head.

New Kingdom from disastrous inflation. No degree of piety, however, could keep these treasures out of circulation at a time when Egyptians were suffering from a dramatic reversal in their fortunes. Late in the Twentieth Dynasty, the mayor of western Thebes, a man named Pewera, was actually accused of cooperating with the grave robbers. Western Thebes was the site of the Valley of Kings and of the great necropolises of the New Kingdom, so Pewera had more dead constituents than live ones, and guarding their welfare was a major part of his responsibilities. Astonishingly, Pewera managed to stay in office despite overwhelming evidence of his complicity. His

accuser, the mayor of eastern Thebes, fared worse. He was reprimanded for having pressed the charges in the first place.

By this time, little was left of the burial wealth of the great New Kingdom pharaohs. Hoping to save the royal mummies that had been left behind in the opened and despoiled tombs, the priests of Thebes resorted to desperate measures. One group of mummies was hidden in an inconspicuous cave in the cliffs of Deir-el-Bahri. Another cache of bodies was stuffed into the tomb of Amenhotep II. Ironically, these hasty reburials survived undisturbed until the late nineteenth century.

Queen Karomama (left), consort of the Twenty-second Dynasty pharaoh Osorkon I from Lybia, had this statue of bronze inlaid with gold and silver fashioned for her chapel at Karnak. Right, a statue of Amon; though theoretically invisible, this Theban god was here portrayed in human form.

Pyramid building survived into Roman and early Christian times at Meroe, south of the Fifth Cataract (below), giving evidence of Egypt's strong influence on the civilization of Nubia.

They might have rested in peace even longer had local villagers not been tempted by the growing demand for antiquities on the part of European collectors. Members of one Theban family, the Rasuls, discreetly looted the Deir-el-Bahri mummies of their jewelry for a number of years, selling the treasures through dealers in nearby Luxor. Suspicious officials were finally able to draw a confession out of one of the Rasuls, who led them to a distinguished company of corpses that included Thutmose III, Seti I, and Rameses II. The mummies were carefully removed from their cave for one last journey down the Nile—this time to the Cairo Museum.

By the end of the Twenty-first Dynasty, the colossus of the Nile was moribund. The last native-born pharaoh ruled as late as 341 B.C., but for much of the six-hundred-year period between the end of the Twenty-first Dynasty and that date, Egypt was ruled either by conquerors or by assimilated foreigners. The Twenty-second Dynasty, for example, was founded by Sheshonq, an Egyptianized Libyan who led an invasion of Palestine that resulted in the sacking of Jerusalem.

More singular still was the Twenty-fifth Dynasty reign of an Ethiopian prince named Piankhi, who ruled the independent and increasingly powerful kingdom of Kush to the south. Piankhi's career is a measure of how thoroughly Nubia and Kush had been permeated by Egyptian culture. In about 730 B.C., he led his mounted troops out of Napata, the Kushite capital near the Fourth Cataract, north into Egypt proper and set about restoring forms of art, worship, and writing characteristic of earlier periods. This desert prince, whose love of Egyptian history was rivaled only by his passion for horses, was not so much a reformer as a purist.

Nevertheless, his zeal struck a responsive chord in an establishment that longed for the restoration of past glories. Piankhi and his descendants of the Twenty-fifth Dynasty were by no means barbarians. In fact, they understood Egyptian culture so well that some Egyptologists hold that Piankhi was a descendant of the Amonite priest Herihor, who ruled during the Twenty-first Dynasty. Unlikely as it seems, the Kushites were accepted in Egypt. They were no match, however, for the armies of the Assyrian Empire that swept the Nile Valley around 670 B.C. and chased the Ethiopians all the way back to their Napatan homeland.

Even after the Assyrians had departed, leaving behind a native-born vassal named Psamtik to guard this outpost of their overextended empire, Egypt still did not manage to shake off its fascination with the past. Psamtik's family, the Saites, instituted a minor renaissance. Though Saite artists were highly skilled, they devoted their energies to copying earlier works, often with such fidelity that it is difficult to tell their copies from the originals. The Saites also revitalized trade, establishing Egyptian grain imports as the mainstay of the Mediterranean economy. One Saite king, Necho, launched an ambitious expedition that attempted to circumnavigate Africa. Nevertheless, most of this business was carried out by foreigners under grants from the crown, and foreigners were reaping the profits. In 525 B.C., Egypt was overrun by the Persians, and its life as an independent power was over. After a brief revival of native rule, the Nile kingdom fell once again—this time to Alexander the Great.

Under the Persians, the Greeks, and eventually the Romans, Egypt continued to be a rich agricultural region. Egyptian antiquities still had their share of admirers, especially among the Greeks, who were under the impression that the gods of the Nile were older and more venerable versions of their own deities. At this time, however, the Egyptian people had become foreigners in their own country, cut off from their heritage, misunderstood, and often actively despised. They would not regain control of their own destiny until the twentieth century.

Alexander and the World of Hellenism

In the year 332 B.C., the newly installed pharaoh of Egypt announced that he was "passionately eager" to visit the shrine of Amon at Siwa, an oasis in the Libyan desert. The pharoah and his armed escort first marched west along the Mediterranean coast, then turned south into the interior. Somehow, the guides became confused and struck a course that drifted west of the proper route. When a southerly wind enveloped the travelers in a blinding sandstorm, they might well have perished had not a pair of snakes magically appeared to lead them to Siwa, "hissing as they went."

The question the pharaoh brought to the priest-oracle of Amon was so sensitive that he refused to share it with his most trusted confidants. Even upon emerging from the sanctuary, he told no one what had transpired except that he had received "the answer his heart desired." The incident, a subject of tantalizing speculation over the centuries, would most likely have been forgotten if it had been insti-

gated by anyone but this young pharaoh. His titles were the usual ones: "Horus," "the Strong Prince," "Beloved of Amon and Selected of Re," "He Who Laid Hands on the Lands of the Foreigners." Yet the pharaoh was himself a foreigner without a drop of Egyptian blood. He had arrived in the Nile Valley as King Alexander III of Macedon, and only a few months after becoming pharaoh he left to pursue yet another title: "Lord of All Asia."

Alexander the Great spent little more than six months in Egypt and conquered the Nile without fighting a single battle. Ten years earlier, the collapse of a nationalist revolt had sent the last native-born pharaoh, Nectanebo II, fleeing to Ethiopia; now, a people weary of Persian domination hailed the Macedonian conqueror as a liberator. Alexander was careful to cultivate his popularity among the Egyptians. He offered sacrifices at the temple of the sacred bull Apis and adopted the crown and regalia of the traditional rulers of the Two Lands. But he also set his personal stamp on the Nile Valley. He carefully selected the site for a new capital, which was destined to become the greatest of a series of Alexandrias built throughout the known inhabited world.

A Greek presence in Asia's cities was nothing new, for the Greeks had long been known as avid colonizers

and skillful mercenaries. But in a reign of only thirteen years, Alexander succeeded in disseminating Greek language, culture, civic institutions, and, above all, garrisons from Anatolia to Egypt and from Syria to Central Asia. In one sense, Alexander was an anachronism—a soldier who had modeled himself on the epic heroes of the long-vanished Homeric age. But he was also a visionary. Born into a culture that distinguished clearly between Greek and barbarian, he saw the possibility of admitting at least some foreigners into the select company of Greek society.

The personal empire Alexander built did not survive intact after his death, but even in dissolution it gave birth to the Hellenistic kingdoms that dominated the Mediterranean world for three hundred years, until the triumph of imperial Rome. Those three centuries were violent ones, marked by cultural dislocation and rampant opportunism. But they were also an age of material opulence and intellectual ferment, as Alexander's heirs tested their talents and aspirations on the stage of the vastly expanded world he bequeathed to them.

In death, Alexander the Great cast a long shadow, but even during his lifetime there were those to whom his successes seemed superhuman. He himself was among the first to wonder whether his accomplish-

Opening page, the ruins of Pella. The settlement was once an outpost of Classical Greek culture in the midst of an archaic society.

Facing page, the valley of the Vardar, a typically rugged landscape of upper Macedonia.

Above, a high mountain pass between Macedonia and Thessaly, the rich province annexed by Philip II. The stone pillars of Thessaly's Meteora plain (right) were thought to have been flung to earth during a battle of the gods.

Pebble mosaics (above), composed of specially prepared colored stones sometimes separated by lead strips, were used to decorate the floor of the men's dining room. Pella, despite its reputation for provincialism, boasted some fine examples of this nascent art form.

ments were not proof of his divine nature. In accepting the pharaonic title Son of Amon, Alexander was merely practicing good politics, but his pilgrimage to Siwa, a shrine not normally associated with Egyptian royalty, went beyond the bounds of shrewd propaganda: Perhaps he secretly wished for confirmation of his divine origins. The god worshiped at Siwa was actually Zeus-Amon, a composite divinity who had been well-known in the Greek world for over a century. For a Greek to claim to be "Zeus-sprung" was nothing new, yet to take such claims about oneself too seriously was an invitation to ridicule.

The twenty-four-year-old king had already had reason to speculate about his ancestry. His parents both claimed direct descent from Zeus, and his mother, Olympias, belonged to a family that was said to have been founded upon the marriage of Achilles' son, Neoptolemus, to Andromache, the widow of Hector. As a boy of shorter-than-average stature, Alexander had found this connection with the heroic Achilles a great comfort. His days were devoted to hardening his body with military exercises. He dressed in simple, thin clothing and ate scanty meals. He also loved to read, and at night he slept with a copy of the *Iliad* under his pillow next to his dagger, a practice he observed his entire life.

This much of Alexander's heritage was universally accepted, but it seems likely that the mystically inclined Olympias hinted to her son that his relationship to Zeus was more direct. Furious over her husband's affairs, Olympias spread rumors that she had once been favored by a divine lover. The most widely accepted tale, probably invented by the queen herself, was that Alexander's conception had been the

Above left, Demosthenes, the Athenian orator who denounced Philip's ambitions in a series of speeches known as the Philippics.

Above right, a gold coin bearing the portrait of Philip II.

Right, Dionysus riding a leopard, a fine example of a mosaic pavement from a Pellan home of the late fourth or early third century B.C.

result of intercourse with a serpent. Another legend said that the queen was struck at the moment of conception by a thunderbolt in the womb, from which fires spread to envelope the whole world.

After Siwa, Alexander's closest followers felt that the king's growing preoccupation with his own divinity set a dangerous precedent. One of these was Callisthenes, a nephew of Aristotle. After having worked on a laudatory history of the Macedonians' campaigns, Callisthenes is supposed to have said of Alexander, "Alexander's fame depends on me and my history and not on the lies which Olympias spread about his parentage."

Whatever Alexander may have believed when he reached Egypt, his original inspiration was certainly neither Zeus nor Achilles but his mortal father, Philip II of Macedon. Macedon was a poor country even by Greek standards, and when Philip came to the throne, his entire wealth is said to have consisted of a single gold cup. The Macedonians themselves were a hard-fighting hill people who spoke a dialect of Greek. Their traditions were more tribal than civic, with the king exercising power as the leader of a court of nobles who were known as *hetaroi*, or companions.

A century earlier, during the Persian Wars, the Macedonians had been forced to ally themselves with

93

Above, the reverse of a gold stater minted by Philip II. After annexing the rich mines of Mount Pangaeus in Thrace in 356 B.C., Philip issued the first regular gold coinage in Europe.

The Lion of Amphipolis (right) commemorates Philip's success in wresting that strategically located city from Athenian control.

Philip celebrated his victory at Chaeronea (338 B.C.) by building the Philippeion at Olympia (below). The circular edifice contained portrait statues of the Macedonian royal family by Leochares.

Darius I and Xerxes, even though sympathies of the Macedonian king lay with the Greeks; the Greeks returned the favor by dismissing Macedon as less than civilized. Alexander I, "the Philhellene," won Macedonian independence by betraying his Persian overlords, and he eventually gained admission to the Olympic Games, which signaled his acceptance as a genuine Greek. He then made a further bid for respectability by welcoming such notable Greeks as Pindar and Herodotus to his court. His grandson Archelaus continued this tradition by establishing a Greek-style capital at Pella.

By the time Philip came to the throne in 359 B.C., Macedon had developed both economically and politically, and Philip himself was cultured enough to admire Euripides and to choose Aristotle as a tutor for Alexander. Philip was, above all, a military genius. By a combination of incessant warfare and shrewd diplomacy, he extended the boundaries of his kingdom to include Thrace in the east and Thessaly in the south. He longed to become the leader of all Greece, yet his most vocal opponent, the Athenian orator Demosthenes, would never let him forget his Macedonian origins. To him, Philip was "a Macedonian villain, from that country...where once we scorned to buy slaves."

The chief instrument of Philip's ambition was the Macedonian army. The heavy infantry, or phalanx, was organized on a revolutionary principle, based on closely marshaled yet maneuverable formations of soldiers who wielded long spears, or *sarissas,* graded in lengths of up to fourteen feet. The Macedonian cavalry was also unexcelled, as might be expected, considering the national passion for horsemanship. Perhaps most important, Philip's army was not only superbly trained but also capable of making war year-round.

Sparta, which possessed the only standing army in Greece, managed to evade Philip's thirst for domination. The other two major holdouts were Athens and Thebes. Demosthenes encouraged the Thebans to make a stand against the Macedonian army by renouncing a treaty they had previously signed, but when Philip's troops met the allies at the battle of Chaeronea in 338 B.C., the promised Athenian support did not amount to much. Though Demosthenes fled the fray to denounce Philip another day, the Theban elite infantry, the hitherto unbeaten Sacred Band, was surrounded and died to the last man.

Philip had no desire to destroy the Greek cities. He did intend to lead them, however, through the mechanism of the League of Corinth, which he formed shortly after Chaeronea and which promptly elected him Supreme Commander of the combined Greek

This Hellenistic coin (above) portrays Alexander wearing the lion-skin headgear of Heracles.

Right, a Macedonian temple on the Sacred Way to Delphi. Philip liberated the sanctuary of Apollo from its occupation by the Phocians.

The myth of Alexander

The character of Alexander the Great is a riddle that every generation reviews in the light of its own experiences with absolute power. In this century, Alexander has been compared both with Hitler and with Stalin and praised as a prophet of universal brotherhood and racial harmony. The interpretations are modern, but they reflect contradictions that troubled Alexander's contemporaries.

His personal valor aside, the young conqueror had many inspiring qualities. He was, for example, a generous friend and a tireless worker. He had a keen intellect and an inquiring mind. The king's flirtation with "oriental" ways, however, inspired scandalous stories as well as more damaging suspicions that he had gone mad. Symptomatic of his imbalance were the occasions when he murdered some of his closest friends on slight provocation. By the end of his life, there is little question that his exercise of power was arbitrary, even ruthless.

Aristotle (above left) became Alexander's tutor when the prince was thirteen years old, and encouraged his wide-ranging curiosity. Above right, Alexander meets Diogenes the Cynic in Corinth. Diogenes is said to have practiced self-sufficiency while living in a large barrel. Tradition says that when Alexander offered to grant the philosopher a favor Diogenes replied: "Step aside a little then, you are blocking the sun."

Facing page, a portrait of Alexander from Pergamon, ca. 160 B.C. Below left, a Macedonian horseman, portrayed on a fragment of a sarcophagus showing one of the Macedonian princes who accompanied young Alexander on hunting expeditions near Pella. Below right, Alexander taming his horse Bucephalus in a bronze statuette of Hellenistic-Etruscan provenance. Alexander's ability to break and ride a horse was a highly reputed accomplishment. His loyalty to Bucephalus was so complete that he named a city in the horse's honor.

This mosaic from a private house in Pella, ca. 300 B.C., recalls a lion hunt organized by the king of Sidon for the Macedonian officers. A noble Macedonian (shown at right), sometimes thought to be Craterus, comes to assist Alexander. Craterus was to become one of the king's leading generals.

armies. Philip was then in a position to carry out his second daring plan: the liberation of the Greek cities of Asia Minor from Persian rule. Macedon would, of course, be the primary beneficiary of such a campaign, but Philip still longed for acceptance as a Greek patriot, and he was careful to present his goal in a way that would appeal to the Athenians. Officially, the war was a campaign to restore Greek honor, avenging the sacking of the Athenian Acropolis by Xerxes in 480 B.C. Considering Macedon's past alliances—not to mention later charges that Demosthenes was in the pay of the Persians—this call to arms was not without its ironies. But the desire for

revenge against the "barbarians" of Persia was still strong in many Greek hearts, and although the troops were recruited almost entirely from Macedonia, Thrace, Illyria, and other regions that had little cause to defend the honor of Athens, the myth soon took on a force of its own.

But before Philip could launch his crusade, he had to attend to some problems at home. Philip was emphatically polygamous and Alexander, disturbed by Philip's treatment of Olympias, had become convinced that his father planned to cheat him of his right to inherit the throne. This quarrel, which broke out just as Philip had managed to establish a states-

manlike image abroad, shows a different side of the Macedonian king. The hard-drinking, battle-scarred veteran had, as the saying went, "a wife for every campaign" and a court rife with favorites, male and female. The question of succession came into the open at Philip's latest wedding when Attalus, an uncle of the bride, sneeringly suggested that the union might result in a "legitimate" heir. Alexander naturally took exception to this remark, which led to a shouting match with his father. According to some accounts, Philip drew his sword, but he was so drunk that a lunge in his son's direction sent him sprawling.

This incident resulted in exile for both Alexander

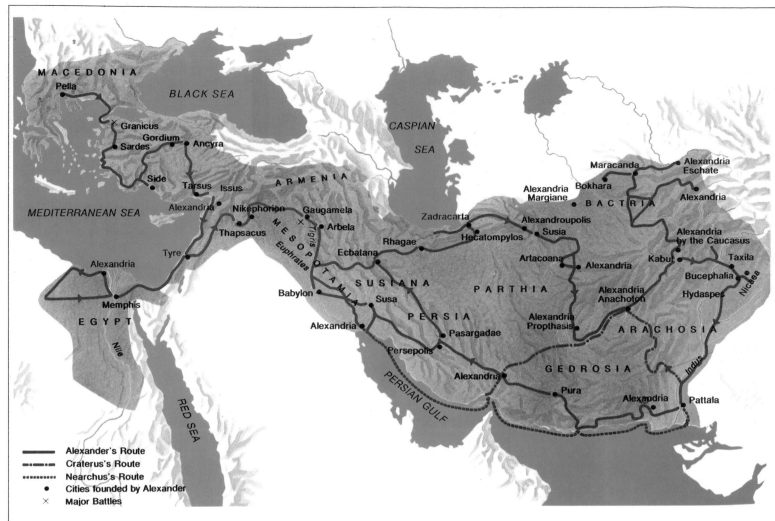

MACEDONIA
Pella
BLACK SEA
× Granicus
Gordium
Sardes • Ancyra
Side
Tarsus
Issus
CASPIAN
SEA
Alexandria
ARMENIA
Nikephorion Gaugamela
Maracanda
Alexandria
Eschate
Alexandria
Margiane Bokhara
BACTRIA
Alexandria
Thapsacus
× Arbela
Zadracarta
Alexandroupolis
Alexandria
by the Caucasus
MEDITERRANEAN SEA
Tyre
Euphrates MESOPOTAMIA Ecbatana
Rhagae
Hecatompylos
Susia
Artacoana
Alexandria
Kabul
Taxila
Bucephalia
Alexandria SUSIANA
Babylon
Susa
PERSIA
Memphis
EGYPT
Nile
Alexandria
Pasargadae
PARTHIA
Alexandria
Anachoton
Alexandria
Propthasis
Hydaspes
Nicaea
ARACHOSIA
Persepolis
Alexandria
GEDROSIA
Indus
PERSIAN GULF
Alexandria
Pura
Alexandria
Pattala
RED SEA

— Alexander's Route
—·—·— Craterus's Route
·········· Nearchus's Route
• Cities founded by Alexander
× Major Battles

The map above gives an overview of Alexander's entire campaign.

The long march

"A ruler should not only be better than his subjects," wrote the Greek general Xenophon, "he should cast a spell over them." Few kings have fulfilled this maxim better than Alexander the Great. When he left Macedonia in 334 B.C., the young king was in debt, having borrowed to complete the outfitting of his troops. Eleven years later, he ruled an empire of some two million square miles.

Alexander's expedition into Asia was an extraordinary achievement. Greek historians hailed it as the crowning glory of Macedonian exploits in the wars against the Persians, and Alexander has come to be most famed as the conqueror of the Persian Empire—and of a large part of the known world of his day. But there were other less obvious marvels. Scholars calculate that the Macedonian forces traversed over fifteen thousand miles, much of which was desert or mountainous. Behind the long list of victories lies the solution to the enormous problems of supplying and quartering troops through the winters of ten long years on the road, from the spring of

334 B.C. until February of 324 B.C.

After Alexander's death, the empire began to disintegrate, but his legend continued to flourish. In Egypt, storytellers claimed that the conqueror was the son of their last native-born pharaoh, Nectanebo II, who was said to have visited Olympias disguised as an astrologer. Predicting that the queen would bear a child to Amon, Nectanebo duly returned, dressed as a god, to fulfill his own prophecy.

The Persians, meanwhile, said that Olympias had once been married to Darius III, who returned her to Epirus after the wedding night because her bad breath repelled him; Olympias cured the condition by chewing sikander (chervil) and, when she gave birth to Darius's son, named the child after the remedy. Tales of Sikander's heroic deeds circulated in the Middle East for centuries.

The Azara Herm (left) is one of the official portraits of Alexander. The bronze original of this Roman copy was sculpted by Lysippus, who followed Alexander on his Asian expedition.

Center right, a statue, found at Luxor, of Alexander in the traditional stance and costume of a traditional pharaoh.

Clockwise from top left, panoramic vistas from the Macedonians' "long march": the strait of the Dardanelles; the Taurus Mountains; the Euphrates; (left) a salt flat in the Persian desert and (right) the Sarang Pass, which leads to the valley of the Oxus (Amu Darya), the river that forms the frontier between Afghanistan and Soviet Central Asia; the ruins of the South Palace of Babylon; and the coast of the Persian Gulf.

Above left, the first phase of Alexander's march, from the crossing of the Hellespont in the spring of 334 B.C. to the fall of Tyre two years later.

Above right, the acropolis of Assos near Troy. It was in this region that Alexander paid homage to his hero Achilles.

Below, the Taurus Mountains.

and Olympias. Unlike his mother, Alexander was soon summoned home, but matters were never the same again between father and son. Mistrust surfaced once again when Alexander, under the no doubt mistaken impression that Philip planned to leave the throne to Arrhidaeus, his mentally retarded son by another wife, tried to interfere with plans for the hapless boy's wedding. Alexander was forgiven a second time, but the truce did not prevent Philip from

Above, the ruins of Priene, one of the principal cities of Ionia, which stood near the foot of Mount Mycale. Characteristically, Alexander restored its democratic civic institutions after he took the city from the Persians.

arranging a third wedding—this one between his daughter Cleopatra and her uncle, the king of Epirus. This union appeared to be the long-sought solution to the meddlesome inference of Philip's queen; now that Philip's new wife provided the needed link with Epirus, Olympias's influence could be permanently eliminated from the court.

For the day of the ceremonies, Philip had planned a session of athletic games. Not wanting his Greek guests to think him a tyrant, he arranged to enter the festivities without his usual bodyguard—a fatal gesture. As Philip approached the ceremonial throne to preside over the contests, Pausanias, one of his own bodyguards, suddenly drew a knife and stabbed the old king in the chest.

Pausanias had a long-standing grievance to redress. Once Philip's lover, an honorable relationship in itself, Pausanias had been accused of goading a younger rival into throwing away his life in battle—in defense of Philip. The young man had been a relative of Attalus, who took revenge on Pausanias by getting him hopelessly drunk and turning him over to his slaves for homosexual rape. Pausanias had appealed to Philip, but rather than punishing Attalus, the king proceeded to marry the adversary's niece. Sordid as this story was, many people then and since have been

convinced that there was a more sinister motive for the regicide. Some have suspected Alexander and Olympias of having revived Pausanias's antagonism. Ultimately, the Greeks regarded Philip's assassination as an unsolved crime—and so it remains today.

Alexander moved quickly to assign the blame to his enemies. Later, he claimed that the murder had been planned by paid agents of the Persians. At the time, he used the occasion to eliminate troublesome enemies and rivals. Attalus was executed, and his niece, Philip's newest bride, was murdered along with her infant child. By Macedonian custom, no king could be crowned without acclamation by the army, but Alexander soon won the support of Antipater and Parmenion, Philip's field marshals.

Alexander had held his first battlefield command at the age of sixteen. Now, at twenty, he moved with the decisiveness of a seasoned commander. He soon

Battle of the Granicus

"It was a cavalry battle with, as it were, infantry tactics: horse against horse, man against man, locked together...." Arrian's vivid description of the Battle of the Granicus in the spring of 334 B.C., compiled from contemporary sources more than four centuries later, describes the action as a test of cavalries.

The heavy Persian cavalry, trusting in its numerical strength, attempted to overrun the Macedonian center. In the ensuing confusion, Alexander was wounded in a duel with one of the Persian chiefs. With typical rashness, he rushed straight back into the fray, and his life was saved only by the intervention of his friend Clitus. But the Persian attack on the Macedonian center came to nothing, while Alexander's Macedonian cavalry charged on both wings, converged on the center, and encircled the enemy.

Mounted units were considered the strong point of both forces, but the highly disciplined Macedonians, armed with sturdy correl wood lances that could be used again and again in close combat, proved superior to the Persian horsemen, who, once they had thrown their javelins, were reduced to defending themselves with their daggers.

The Granicus was a decisive victory for the Macedonians. It clearly demonstrated the versatility of Alexander's war machine as well as the courage of its commander and his strategic skill. Alexander used the triumph as an occasion to flatter his Greek allies and reprove the recalcitrant citizens of Sparta who had refused him aid. After the battle he awarded three hundred sets of captured Persian armor to the Athenians, and the gift was accompanied by an inscription that pointedly gave credit for his success to the Greeks—"except the Spartans."

Below, Alexander on the charging Bucephalus. This bronze statuette is from the Naples Museum.

marched south, had himself elected to his father's former post, head of the League of Corinth, then led a major expedition into formerly unexplored territory north of the Danube. A true test of the young king's mettle came from Thebes, his father's old enemy. Encouraged by the Athenian Demosthenes and by a widespread rumor of Alexander's death, the Thebans armed themselves for rebellion. News of the revolt reached Alexander in Illyria, and fourteen days later, much to the Thebans' surprise, he appeared outside their walls. The victory that followed was one of the most destructive of Alexander's whole career. Thebes was razed and the entire population was killed or sold into slavery. Only the temples and the house of Pindar were spared.

It is possible, as Alexander's apologists later claimed, that his Greek allies enthusiastically led in the sacking of their more powerful neighbor; nonetheless, it was Alexander who benefited. With his opponents in Greece temporarily crushed, he was now free to carry out the Persian campaign long planned by his father. An advance force under Parmenion was already in Asia Minor. And in the spring of 334 B.C., Alexander ignored the plea of his chosen viceroy Antipater, who had urged him to marry and beget an heir before leaving home, and set out across the Hellespont.

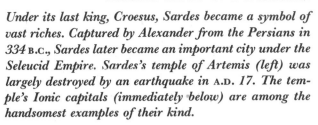

Under its last king, Croesus, Sardes became a symbol of vast riches. Captured by Alexander from the Persians in 334 B.C., Sardes later became an important city under the Seleucid Empire. Sardes's temple of Artemis (left) was largely destroyed by an earthquake in A.D. 17. The temple's Ionic capitals (immediately below) are among the handsomest examples of their kind.

The tortuous route of the Maeander River (left), as it makes its way from Phrygia to the Aegean Sea, gave the word "meandering" to the English language. The valley was vital to the control of the coast south of Ephesus, and Alexander garrisoned it with a force of fifteen hundred men at Celaenae.

The confidence with which this campaign against Asia was launched may have seemed naive in light of the vast extent of the Persian territory. Indeed, the number of Greek mercenaries alone in the service of the Persian king was said to equal the size of Alexander's whole army. Nevertheless, the Hellenes' confidence may have been justified. The Achaemenid dynasty ruled its far-flung domains through *satraps,* or aristocratic governors, who were often out of contact with the Great King for months at a time. Although records are scanty, we know that the Achaemenids had been troubled by widespread rebellion. Their court was riddled with intrigue, and the new Great King, Darius III, was a usurper who had come to power after a spate of poisonings engineered by a palace eunuch. Moreover, as Alexander must have known from his study of Herodotus and Xenophon, the Persian army was notoriously unwieldly, an ideal target for his highly coordinated army and especially for the elite Companion Cavalry, which could descend with lightning speed on an enemy's weak points. Counting the troops of his Greek allies, Alexander's force totaled fewer than fifty thousand. His fleet amounted to only 160 ships, and even this he soon disbanded, saying that he would "defeat the Persian fleet on land."

Yet the Macedonians had one advantage that would prove to be decisive: Their officers had been trained in the military life from birth. While the Persian aristocracy surrounded itself with luxuries, the Macedonians considered even warm baths an indulgence suitable only for pregnant women. Far from being barbarians in our sense of the word, the Persians were, if anything, overcivilized. In the end, even their most practical achievement, the Royal Road stretching from Anatolia to the heart of Asia, served Alexander's well-disciplined, fast-moving army better than it did their own.

The Macedonians' Asian campaign opened with a symbolic gesture, calculated to emphasize Alexander's spiritual links with the heroes of the *Iliad.* Making straight for Troy, Alexander honored his ancestor by stripping nude for a ceremonial race to Achilles' tomb. Hephaestion, Alexander's closest friend, is said to have laid a wreath on the tomb of Patroclus, a close friend of Achilles.

This gesture, touchingly expressive of a relationship that ended with Hephaestion's death only months before Alexander's own, was unfortunately a prelude to a battle that pitted Greek against Greek. The Persian army that met the Macedonians at the Granicus River included a large force of Greek mercenaries under a general named Memnon, himself a

Mute for over a century and a half, the oracle of Apollo at Didyma supposedly broke its silence upon the approach of the Macedonian army when it uttered a single word—"Alexander." A new temple of Apollo (above) was begun during the reign of Seleucus I to replace the temple destroyed by the Persians in 494 B.C. This second temple was one of the grandest Greek temples in Asia Minor.

The Hellenistic taste for elaborate decorative motifs is revealed in the base of this column fragment (left). The Medusa's head (right) was originally part of the temple façade.

Greek. Memnon knew his enemy, and he advised the Persian satraps to pursue a scorched earth policy. He was overruled. Ironically, the Persian rout that followed was most costly for the Greeks, who did not even have a chance to enter the fight. Denouncing them as traitors to a patriotic cause, Alexander had them rounded up; many were killed, and the rest were shipped back to slavery in Macedonia.

As both this action and the destruction of Thebes proved, Alexander could be ruthless when he deemed it to be necessary. On the other hand, he had little taste for gratuitous slaughter. A brilliant combat commander, he was also attentive to the day-to-day business of leadership. The first-century A.D. historian Arrian, who based his work on contemporary accounts of Alexander's conquests, describes the king's "deep concern" for the wounded after the Battle at the Granicus, noting that he visited them all, "allow-

ing [each man] to tell his story and exaggerate as much as he pleased."

When it came to consolidating territory already won, Alexander was equally thorough. In the cities of Asia Minor, Alexander assured his welcome by overthrowing Persian-supported oligarchies in favor of democracy. He also abolished Persian taxes, and although the Macedonians naturally imposed new levies, these were diplomatically called "contributions to the army of liberation." At Ephesus, the citizens actually threw open the gates of the city and welcomed the Macedonians as heroes. The army's progress was not always this easy; the fortified city of Halicarnassus put up especially stiff resistance under the leadership of Memnon. But as winter closed in, Alexander felt secure enough to grant furloughs to all Macedonian troops who had married shortly before the campaign began—a policy that must have ben-

Ephesus (facing page), once the busiest port in Asia Minor, threw open its gates to the Macedonian army. Above, a horse from the mausoleum of Halicarnassus. One of the Seven Wonders of the Ancient World, the tomb was built for King Mausolus in 353 B.C. Right, excavated ruins at Gordium where Alexander is said to have untied the famous knot. Below, the valley of Goreme in Cappadocia, another region claimed by Alexander.

Battle of Issus

Having been reared on Xenophon's fictionalized account of the life of Cyrus the Great, Alexander must have approached Issus hoping that Darius III would be, if not another Cyrus, at least a worthy foil for his own legend. In any event, Darius failed to live up to his imposing physical presence, and Alexander's chroniclers were quick to blame the Persian defeat on the Great King's overconfidence and on the courtiers who "blew up his conceit."

Yet the Great King's loss at Issus in 333 B.C. was not as ignominious as these accounts suggest. The chroniclers' claim that the Persian army numbered six hundred thousand men was a wild exaggeration. Actually, the two forces were well matched, and as the Persian infantry was composed largely of untrained recruits, the Macedonians may well have held the advantage.

Curiously enough, the most determined troops on the Persian side were Greek mercenaries, who drove a wedge through the heart of the Macedonian formation. When Alexander rushed to the center, he left his own wing undefended, effectively handing Darius his chance for victory. But the Great King misjudged the situation, panicked, and fled the field.

The battle of Issus was the turning point in this great clash between East and West. Not surprisingly, it became the favorite theme of Hellenistic artists. The supposed face-to-face confrontation between Alexander and his arch rival Darius is commemorated in the largest surviving mosaic from ancient times, discovered at Pompeii in 1831. The battle scenes (above and preceding page) are thought to be based on the work of the Greek painter Philoxenos of Eretria.

efited the Macedonian birthrate as much as it did his own popularity.

In the spring of 333 B.C., the army regrouped at Gordium, capital of the legendary King Midas and site of the Gordian knot, the leather thong that held together the yoke and shaft of a venerable old wagon said to have carried Midas himself. A local prophecy foretold that whoever untied the knot would become the ruler of all Asia. Naturally, Alexander's historians all agree that he passed this symbolic test, but there are many different versions of how. One tale, consistent with Alexander's character, is that he simply drew his sword and sliced through the thong, announcing, "Now I have untied it."

Despite this favorable omen, the Macedonians were overextended. They had reached the end of the Greek-inhabited territory of Asia Minor and were approaching lands in which they had no friendly contacts. Worse still, Alexander had pushed himself to the point of physical exhaustion. At Tarsus, after bathing in the waters of the Cydnus, he fell ill with a

Details from the largest surviving mosaic show Alexander (above) confronting Darius III (preceding pages) at the battle of Issus. Below, a dying Persian, sculpted at Pergamon in the third century B.C.

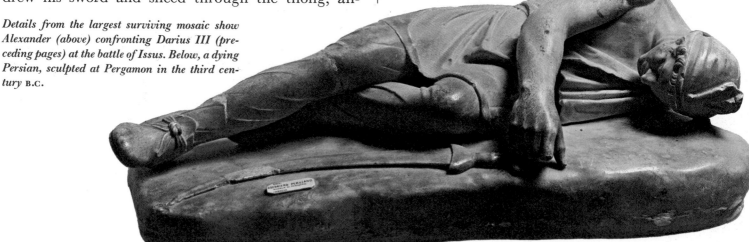

fever, and the army's advance was delayed pending his recovery. While Alexander's life hung in the balance, the Great King of the Persians, the six-and-one-half-foot-tall Darius III, had finally bestirred himself and was moving west through Syria at the head of an enormous force.

When the Macedonians finally resumed their advance, the two armies actually crossed paths, and Darius, approaching the Bay of Issus by an inland route, surprised himself by capturing a field hospital that had been set up for the wounded of Alexander's army. Darius rose to the occasion by ordering that the patients' hands be chopped off. The deed was not Alexander's style, and according to Arrian, he responded to the news by reminding his men in a ringing oration that the Medes and the Persians were "men who for centuries have lived soft and luxurious lives. . . . We are free men," he added, "and they are slaves."

The battle of Issus began with the Persian army bunched into an unpromising position on the narrow

Right, the temple of Byblos in Phoenicia. Its "obelisk" stones were magical symbols of Reshef, god of war. The capture of Tyre (below) after a long and famous siege proved Alexander's tenacity and the superiority of Greek siege equipment.

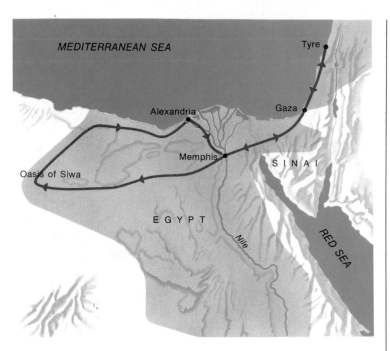

Alexander's progress through Egypt (above) was accomplished without a battle. When the Macedonians reached Memphis in November of 332 B.C., they were welcomed by the people as an alternative to the despised rule of the Persian satrap.

coastal plain, its ranks so deep that the soldiers near the rear would never have a chance to reach the battle lines. At the center stood the towering King of Kings in his gilded war chariot, a tempting target for the Companion Cavalry, led as always by Alexander himself. In an extended battle the Persians might have triumphed, but Darius, overconfident to begin with, was stunned when he saw his right flank crumble under the charge of the swift Macedonian cavalry. Then, seeing Alexander advancing through the ranks of his own bodyguard, Darius panicked and drove his chariot from the field. His flight touched off a general rout, and in the ensuing melee thousands of Persians were trampled by their own men. Darius did not even pause to collect his belongings, and when the victors reached the Persian headquarters, they were stunned by the opulence of Darius's temporary camp. At the sight of the luxurious sofas, gold vessels, and tables set for a postbattle banquet, Alexander may have changed his mind somewhat about the sybaritic tastes of the Persians. "This," he is said to have told his companions, "is what it means to be a king."

The Macedonians soon learned that Darius had left behind more than his furniture. His mother, wife, and three children were also in the camp. The women were terrified, and when Alexander and Hephaestion went to greet them, the Queen Mother blundered by

The pyramids of Giza (left) had been known to educated Greeks for centuries; now, these symbols of eternal Egypt became part of Alexander's personal empire. Above, a funerary stele from the Alexandrian necropolis of Shatby, from the first half of the third century B.C. The image of a Macedonian cavalryman is painted on the stone. Facing page, Alexander, wearing the double crown of Egypt. The young pharaoh offers sacrifices to Amon in this relief from the temple of Luxor.

hailing the taller man as Alexander. The conqueror laughed off the mistake, as he could well afford to do. From the Macedonian point of view, Darius's sin was not so much his desertion of his family as his decadence in bringing the women to the front. Alexander kept the Persian royal women with his army. No doubt he planned to use them eventually as bargaining chips, but his respectful treatment of them also served as a pointed contrast to the Great King's own behavior.

After Issus, the Macedonians swept south along the Mediterranean coast, determined to break the Persians' control of the sea. Alexander's siege of the is-land port of Tyre proved both his brilliance as a tactician and his vindictiveness when opposed. After the city was finally taken following a fierce seven-month resistance, Alexander had all its inhabitants sold into slavery. Having witnessed this example, most of the Phoenician towns surrendered. Only the strategic village of Gaza followed Tyre's example, and when it fell, Alexander was able to march into the Nile Valley unopposed.

Darius, meanwhile, was suing for peace. Parmenion, the elderly field marshal who had served Philip II, is said to have exclaimed on hearing Darius's offer of territory and ransom for his family that if he were

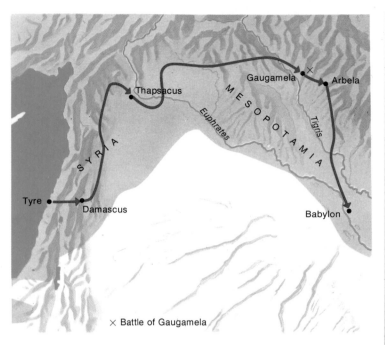

Above, after returning to Tyre in the spring of 331 B.C., Alexander resumed his march along the Persian Royal Road and onward to Gaugamela, where he met Darius III in a final, decisive battle. The route to Gaugamela led across Mesopotamia's twin rivers (facing page): the Euphrates north of present-day Baghdad (above) and the Tigris (below).

Alexander he would surely accept. "So would I," retorted Alexander, "if I were Parmenion. But I am Alexander, so I will send Darius a different message." Alexander's message made clear that he already considered himself master of Darius's kingdom in all but name.

A second battle with Darius was inevitable, but while the Achaemenid king retired beyond the Tigris to gather his forces, Alexander sojourned in Egypt, where he undertook the pilgrimage to the shrine of Amon at Siwa. Alexander was impressed by the riches of the Nile, so much so that he divided control of the country among a number of officers so that none could gain too much power. In the spring of 331 B.C., Alexander moved on, returning to Tyre and marching east across the desert and Mesopotamia. Darius thus had the advantage of meeting the Macedonians on the site of his choice, the broad plain of Gaugamela, where his formidable scythed war chariots could enjoy superior maneuverability. The Persian force was indeed awesome, and Parmenion, always cast by the chroniclers as the voice of caution, is supposed to have urged Alexander to stage a night attack. He refused, scorning the notion of "stealing a victory." Whether the story is true or not, Alexander's apparent brashness once again proved to be based on shrewd analysis. It seems that the Persians had been expecting a night attack. On the day of the battle the Persians fought bravely, but they were weary from their vigil and lacked the organization that distinguished the Macedonians. Alexander ingeniously defeated the threat of the scythed chariots by opposing them with lightly armed foot soldiers, who deftly jumped aside, avoiding the sharp blades projecting from the chariot's wheels. Once again, the battle ended ignominiously for the Persians as Darius drove his chariot from the field and escaped eastward.

Deserted by his Great King, the official Mazaeus surrendered the city of Babylon without a fight. In return, he was made satrap of Babylon, the first time a "barbarian" had been allowed such a high position under Macedonian hegemony. Alexander's army, meanwhile, moved on toward Susa, the former administrative capital of the Persians.

With the acquisition of two Persian treasuries, the king who had gone into debt to get his army out of Macedonia was the richest man in the world. Alexander sent a large sum of money to Antipater, governor of Macedonia, who was preparing for a war with Sparta, gave generously to his friends, and turned some of the Persian gold plate into currency, much of which was distributed to his troops in lieu of the loot they might have had from sacking captured cities.

Only Persepolis, the ceremonial capital of the Achaemenids and the hated symbol of "barbarian" culture, was singled out for destruction. Here, much to the regret of modern archaeologists, Alexander burned the Great King's palace. One story says that this deed grew out of a rather riotous banquet that ended when the Athenian courtesan Thaïs proposed a midnight torch party to repay the Persians for their burning of the Athenian Acropolis 150 years earlier.

In the spring of 330 B.C., the Macedonians moved on to Ecbatana in northwestern Iran. There Alexander learned that Darius and his most powerful supporters were fleeing east into the province of Bactria. Alexander followed as quickly as possible—some sources say his army covered four hundred miles in eleven days—but before he could catch up with Darius, news came that the Great King had been assassinated. No doubt, his once-loyal followers had at last become exasperated by their ruler's vacillation and delays. Alexander was now the undisputed King of Kings, Lord of All Asia.

A century earlier Herodotus had noted that "the Persians admit foreign customs more readily than any other men." This certainly had never been the Greek way of doing things, yet now it was Alexander who began to adopt the customs of the conquered Persians. From this time on, he appeared in public wearing an adaptation of the robes of Persian royalty

Battle of Gaugamela

On October 1, 331 B.C., nearly two years after the battle of Issus, Alexander and Darius III met once again at the battle of Gaugamela. Knowing that Darius's irresolution was his best ally, Alexander offered a sacrifice to Fear on the night before the battle. No doubt the gesture also served to emphasize his own self-confidence, a necessary move since some of the Macedonian troops had thrown down their weapons in panic at the sight of the massed Persian force and had to be exhorted to advance further. Although he faced the Persians with a heavily outnumbered army—about forty-seven thousand men—Alexander still managed to deploy his units effectively against such unfamiliar weapons as scythed chariots and war elephants. He also managed to keep his lines of communication open on a field where swirling dust clouds soon reduced the visibility to zero. With numbers on his side, Darius still lacked, in the words of the military historian E. W. Marsden, "that rare ability to sift conflicting reports . . . remaining cool and unflurried."

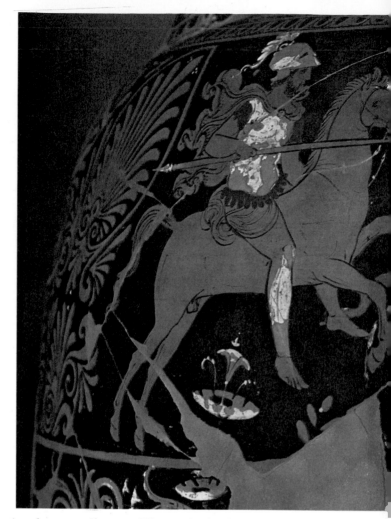

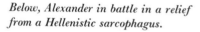

Below, Alexander in battle in a relief from a Hellenistic sarcophagus.

(and, according to Plutarch, in Persian shoes, which allowed for elevator lifts to make the wearer appear taller). Having adamantly refused to take a wife in Macedonia, he soon married the Sogdian princess Roxane, thereby securing the allegiance of all of Sogdiana, where he had been waging a tough guerrilla war for months. He also fell in love with the Persian courtier Bagoas. The match with Roxane was much celebrated in later romances, but this alliance with an eastern princess was hardly popular with Alexander's Macedonian officers, and Bagoas, heartily disliked for being a eunuch, was no more welcome.

Along with Alexander's flirtation with Persian customs came a newfound distrust of his oldest allies. Claiming to uncover a plot among the Companions, Alexander had Philotas, a boyhood friend, executed with a number of other alleged conspirators. Philotas died protesting his innocence—indeed, there seems to have been nothing but circumstantial evidence against him. Unfortunately, this was not the end of the matter. Philotas's father was the marshal Parmenion. Without even granting the old soldier a hearing, Alexander ordered his assassination. The deed can only be justified by assuming that Parmenion would have tried to avenge his son's death. Regardless, it was a sorry end for a loyal officer.

Pragmatist that he was, Alexander saw clearly that

Battlefield encounters between Darius and Alexander were a favorite theme of Hellenistic art. This amphora (above) of the third century B.C. shows a Greek-looking Darius fleeing a bearded Alexander.

Below right, the expressive face of a dying Persian, a Roman copy from the Pergamene monument.

he could never rule Asia through his Macedonian staff alone. There would have to be some integration of Persians and Hellenes. One source of friction between the two groups was *proskynesis,* a Persian custom which involved kneeling or prostrating oneself before the ruler. The Greeks considered such a gesture an appropriate greeting only for a god. The Persians, however, read no religious meaning into this ceremony—by no means did they regard their Great King as a god. This fine point was lost on Alexander's Greek and Macedonian followers. They were convinced that proskynesis implied worship, and when Alexander decided to eliminate inequity by requiring the ceremony of everyone, he must have foreseen how the decision would be interpreted.

Alexander carefully set the stage for his innovation. The ceremony was to be introduced at a banquet by the king's closest friends, all carefully briefed in advance. In return for prostrating himself, each man was to receive the usual fraternal kiss as a conciliatory gesture. The ceremony went smoothly until Callisthenes approached the throne and refused to kneel. Alexander would have ignored the omission if an officious courtier had not insisted on drawing attention to it, but Callisthenes was not about to overlook the refusal of the brotherly embrace he felt was his due. Grumbling that he was "poorer by a kiss," he returned to his seat. That this was enough to turn the tide of opinion suggests how little support proskynesis had, but Callisthenes paid dearly for his opposition. Some time later, he was accused of instigating a plot by the royal pages to assassinate Alexander, and tried for treason. In death, he became a martyr to those who opposed the deification of kings.

Callisthenes's disaffection is perhaps less surprising than the loyalty of the ordinary troops as they pushed toward the most remote corners of the Achaemenid Empire. Alexander continued to establish garrisons and new cities—there were seventeen Alexandrias east of the Euphrates alone, and the last, near Tashkent, was appropriately named Alexandria-the-Farthest. But for many of his soldiers, the campaign must long before have become pointless, and the new lands they marched through were as alien as they were harsh. Crossing the Hindu Kush, the Macedonians encountered terrible snows and heard rumors of a strange people whose oversized feet were attached back to front. In India, the monsoon rains flooded the camp and scores of men were bitten by poisonous water snakes.

The army had become a self-contained "world on

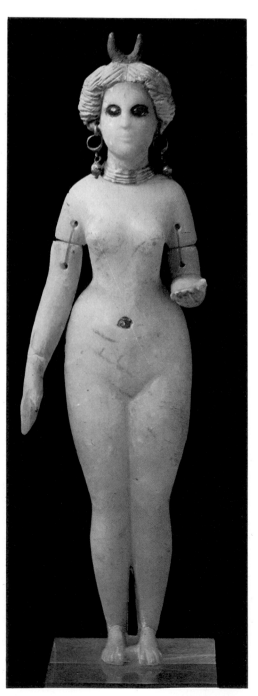

the march," but instead of a triumphal postscript to a long campaign, the conquest of northern India turned out to be a serious affair. One Punjabi king, Porus, used war elephants to neutralize the Macedonian cavalry and fought so bravely that Alexander, after defeating him, made him an ally. Faced with the growing discontent of his troops, Alexander freely distributed booty and made inspiring speeches about the deeds of Heracles. None of this impressed the rank and file, and the general Coenus, an old stalwart, finally came forward as a spokesman for those who wanted to retreat. Hearing his ultimatum, Alexander sulked in his tent for three days, but when the mutineers held firm, he was forced to relent. There, on the Hyphasis (today the Beas River) Alexander had gone as far as he could go. His dream was finished.

Just what Alexander had dreamed of is a matter of some debate. Perhaps he had intended merely to complete his conquest of the Indus region. Perhaps he had heard of the rich kingdom of the Magadha on the Ganges and hoped to conquer it as well. In any case, there could be no thought of leading the army back the way it had come—that course smelled of retreat. Instead, the Macedonians continued to build up the fleet they had begun to develop earlier, when they were still under the impression that the Indus was actually the long-sought source of the Nile. (The confusion had arisen in part from the presence of crocodiles in both rivers.) Now better oriented, Alexander planned to divide his forces, sending the fleet, commanded by Nearchus, through the Persian Gulf, while he and Craterus each commanded a force traveling by land. Leading the troops who were most fit, Alexander chose a coastal route through the barren

Far left, an alabaster figure of the Babylonian goddess Ishtar, inlaid with rubies. Left, the ruins of the Hanging Gardens of Babylon, one of the Seven Wonders of the Ancient World. A lion (above), sacred to Ishtar, guards Babylon's Processional Way. Such reliefs were modeled in wet clay, cut into bricks, and then reassembled after glazing.

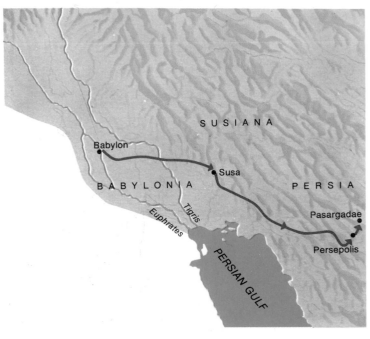

Upon leaving Babylon, Alexander penetrated the heart of the Persian Empire by taking Susa, Persepolis, and Pasargadae in quick succession. He marched unopposed through the region of Fars, the homeland of the Persian people, but there encountered a rugged terrain of both desert (preceding page) and mountain (below).

Facing page, a coin minted at Babylon. Alexander is depicted as a god being crowned by Nike. He holds a Greek cuirass and a thunderbolt of Zeus, but his war helmet shows the influence of a Persian style.

Makran desert. According to Nearchus's history of the journey, Alexander "was not ignorant of the difficulties of the route." But something went drastically wrong. Provisions for the army either were lost or were never organized properly in the first place and the guides lost their way. The desert proved to be inhabited only by primitive tribes, including one, the "Fish-Eaters," who lived in "huts built of shells and roofed with the backbones of fish." Later, the army found itself traversing a trackless wasteland of sand dunes so loosely packed that their mules and horses foundered. Over half of the army and its camp followers, perhaps as many as twenty-five thousand

people, died of thirst or starvation. Nearchus's fleet fared better, but even so, the admiral was so emaciated when he reached the entrance of the Persian Gulf that a search party mistook him for a common beggar.

Whatever else it proved, the march showed that Alexander was far from invincible. Nevertheless, he managed to turn the debacle into a minor victory by spreading a legend, no doubt invented for the occasion, that the Babylonian queen Semiramis had once led an army along the same route and emerged with only twenty survivors.

But for those who had been left behind to govern in

Alexander's absence, his safe return was hardly a blessing. Fearing that many of his appointed satraps had developed too much power, Alexander instituted a purge in 324 B.C. His long-range plans for integrating the administration of his empire continued, however, and in a single mass wedding celebrated at Susa, Alexander saw ten thousand of his veteran soldiers married to Iranian women. The ceremony included the key members of the Macedonian command, who were matched with daughters of the Persian aristocracy. Alexander himself married Barsine, one of the daughters of Darius who had been captured at Issus; and his friend Hephaestion was wed to the other daughter, Drypetis.

Alexander also arranged for thirty thousand Iranian boys to receive a Greek education. Further, he sent memoranda to the Greek cities demanding that they readmit their political exiles and acknowledge his divinity. In general, the first request met with more resistance than the second, although the response to Alexander's divinity was less than enthusi-

astic. "If Alexander wants to be a god, let him be a god," replied the Spartans laconically.

Although it is tempting to examine these actions for signs that they were part of a unified vision of an integrated Greco-Iranian empire, it is likely that Alexander's motives were more pragmatic. He was only thirty-one years old and full of plans. He wanted to explore the Hyrcanium (Caspian) Sea to test the theory that it was actually a gulf of the "Endless Ocean," thought to encircle the known world. He also talked of circumnavigating Arabia. But the young conqueror was increasingly troubled over the prospects of maintaining control of the territory already won. No doubt his demand to be recognized as a god was to some extent calculated to solidify his position. Those who inherited his empire followed his example by choosing to become gods in their own right. In Alexander's case, however, insistence on his godhood seems to have been a symptom of his developing megalomania.

According to the Greek pamphleteer Ephippus,

Above left, a Median archer, from a multi-colored relief at Susa. Above, the ruins of Persepolis in southwest Iran, the ceremonial capital of the Persians. Built largely under Darius I and Xerxes, this national shrine was reduced to ashes by Alexander in 300 B.C. Cyrus the Great's tomb at Pasargadae (right) was looted while Alexander was in India; he ordered it restored and resealed.

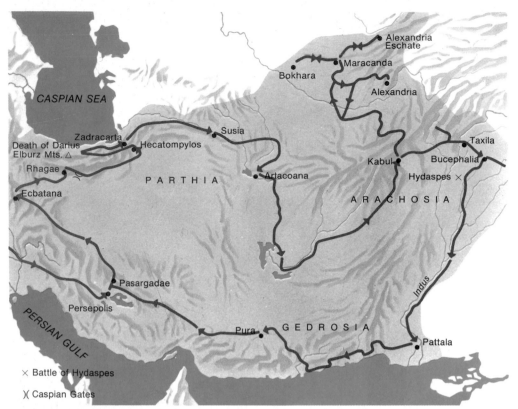

Left, the final stage of Alexander's march, in which Alexander pushed into Afghanistan, reached the foot of the Himalayas, and crossed the Indus. For the return journey to Persia, the army was divided into three parts: Alexander and Craterus each commanded a land force while Nearchus sailed the fleet from the mouth of the Indus to the Persian Gulf.

Below, the Bamian Valley, in Afghanistan, at the foot of the Hindu Kush range.

Alexander had begun to appear in costume wearing the ram's horns and slippers of Amon, the lion-skin loincloth associated with Heracles, as well as the robes of the goddess Artemis. Ephippus's report may have been slander, but his comment that Alexander's temper had grown "murderous and quite unbearable" is supported by friendlier sources. As Arrian put it, the "Oriental subservience to which he had become accustomed had greatly changed his old openhearted manner toward his own countrymen."

In the end, Alexander's plan to discharge ten thousand veterans and replace them with Persians lost him the support of the army. Macedonians who had followed their king to the end of the known world listened in anger to the announcement that they were to be sent home to retirement while control of their proud army was handed over to officers of the people they had defeated. The news touched off a mutiny in the ranks. "Discharge the lot of us and go marching with your Father Amon," the troops shouted.

When Alexander calmly prepared to call their bluff and reorganize his whole army with Persians, the men begged for forgiveness. Alexander pardoned them, celebrating the reconciliation with a banquet at which nine thousand guests, taken from all nations of the kingdom, drank toasts to future harmony. The ten thousand veterans then departed for home under the command of Cratcrus.

Above, a combat scene from a stone relief found near Hadda (northeastern Afghanistan). The subjugation of the rebellious tribes of Sogdiana and Bactria was accomplished only after bloody and extended fighting.

Departing from Bactria in 327 B.C., Alexander crossed the Hindu Kush (right) into India. He undoubtedly followed a route through the mountainous pass of Kaoshan, in central Afghanistan, which lies over 14,000 feet above sea level.

The discovery of crocodiles in the Indus River (left) led Alexander to the mistaken conclusion that he had reached the source of the Nile.

Below, a silver decadrachma, perhaps struck at Babylon. It commemorates the Macedonian victory over King Porus's war elephants at the Jhelum River.

Combat between Greeks and Amazons (facing page) was a popular theme of Hellenistic funerary sculpture. A number of fanciful tales connect Alexander with the Amazons. One story in Plutarch says that the Macedonians encountered a tribe of warrior women in the wilds of Hindu Kush.

A crisis had been averted, but there is little reason to believe that any lasting harmony had been established. Alexander's historians report the beginnings of evil omens at this time. Certainly the worst of these was the sudden death of Hephaestion, and in June of 323 B.C., only weeks after organizing his friend's elaborate funeral, Alexander himself died after a brief illness.

Officially, Alexander's death was attributed to a fever, probably malaria. The story is certainly plausible, for, though a young man, he had already suffered from overwork, battle wounds, and the responsibilities of supreme power. On the other hand, persistent rumors that the conqueror was poisoned by a cabal of former Macedonian supporters indicate, if nothing else, that the mood at his court had turned ugly. Whatever the cause of Alexander's death, there is little doubt that, if he had survived, his sovereignty over the empire he had created would no doubt have been sorely tested.

Only in death could Alexander become all things to all men. In Egypt, legend made him the natural son of the native pharaoh Nectanebo. In the East, he became the romantic hero Sikander. In Europe, he was either the apostle of brotherhood or the archetypal tyrant, depending on the writer's school of

thought. Most immediately, the sudden death of Alexander reinforced the mood of insecurity and disillusionment that already existed in the Hellenic world. Learned Greek writers devoted essays to arguing the question of whether Alexander's accomplishments had been the result of his own superior attrib-

utes or merely a matter of luck. Inconstant Tyche, the goddess of Fortune, became a mesmerizing figure. Demetrius of Phalerum, an Aristotelian, penned this melancholy summary of the careers of Philip and Alexander: "No need to look endlessly through time, generation after generation," he wrote. "The last fifty years show the violence of Fortune. . . . Fortune is not affected by the way we live. . . . At this moment, in establishing the Macedonians in the former glory of the Persians, she is demonstrating that they have those blessings on loan only, till she changes her mind."

It is easy to see why the unexpected inheritance of an empire would inspire a certain amount of anxiety, particularly among those whose cultural background was Greek. But despite Demetrius's assessment, not all Hellenes were pessimistic about their prospects. The rhetorician Isocrates once said, "The name of Hellas [is] distinctive no longer of race but of intellect, and the title of Hellene a badge of education."

In the new order of things, "Hellas" took on a meaning that Isocrates had never intended: Alexander had bequeathed to the Hellenes a new vision of their culture's potential to expand throughout the *oikoumene,* the known inhabited world. He had created a network of Greek cities and garrisons that could form the basis for commercial and cultural empires. To Greek and Macedonian settlers in Bactria or Egypt, the competing local allegiances of their homeland meant little. Greek language and education were the badge of belonging, and even "barbarians"—at least those wealthy enough to attend Greek schools—could become honorary Hellenes. All that was lacking was a political framework for the new Hellenism.

For all his success, Alexander had failed in the one overriding duty of the traditional monarch: He left no recognized heir. The two obvious candidates were Roxane's child, still unborn at Alexander's death, and Arrhidaeus, Alexander's retarded half-brother. The Macedonian soldiery, insisting on its right to acclaim a new king, disliked the idea of being ruled by the child of an Oriental princess; the senior officers

Greco-Oriental art

Brief as it was, Alexander's presence in Asia had lasting repercussions. In northern India the petty king Chandragupta, perhaps directly inspired by Alexander's example, soon conquered the Ganges Valley and established the great Mauryan Empire. Bactria, the ancient kingdom centered in what is now northern Afghanistan, won its independence from the Seleucids but was ruled by a family of Hellenized kings. One of these, a Demetrius, was known to Chaucer as "Emetreus, King of Ynde," and another, in the mid-second century B.C., converted to Buddhism and was later immortalized in an important Buddhist text, "The Questions of King Milinda."

Above, left to right, the varied faces of Greco-Indian art: a stucco head from Gandhara; Athena, portrayed in green schist; a Hadda portrait head, probably of a goddess; and the "genie of flowers," also from Hadda.

Although the actual number of Greek and Macedonian settlers in the East was small, their influence persisted for many generations. The children of Greek immigrants eventually became assimilated, but artists trained in Hellenistic techniques left their mark on the art of the Orient. For example, at Kandahar, formerly Alexandria-in-Arachosia, King Chandragupta's grandson Asoka had Buddhist inscriptions carved in Greek. The Greco-Oriental artists of Gandhara, a region divided between modern Pakistan and Afghanistan, were probably the first to violate the prohibition against creating images of the Buddha. These early portraits of the Enlightened One may have been influenced by the Gandharan artists' familiarity with the serene countenance of Apollo. It is from the original Greco-Oriental statues and reliefs of the Buddha that all Buddhist monumental art has descended.

Right, a Dionysiac revel, Asian style, which combines Greek musical instruments and pottery with typical Oriental poses.

Far right, a low-relief medallion depicting the myth of Ganymede, the beautiful youth chosen by Zeus to serve as his heavenly cupbearer.

could see no merit in Arrhidaeus. Finally, they compromised: There were to be two kings and, since neither was capable of ruling, two regents as well. With the Macedonian generals already beginning to stake out their own territories, this arrangement accomplished little except to guarantee that neither king would live long. (Both were killed in 317 B.C., casualties of a contest between Antipater's son Cassander and Olympias for control of Macedon.)

The most dramatic sign of approaching trouble was the abduction of Alexander's funeral cortege. Embalmed in precious spices and fitted out in a golden sarcophagus, the conqueror's body had been installed inside an ingeniously designed hearse with gold net sides. Pulled by a train of no fewer than sixty-four mules, the shrine began a stately procession to the traditional burial ground of Macedonian kings in Aegae. But when it reached Syria, Alexander's old friend and general Ptolemy conveniently remembered that Alexander had wanted to be buried in Siwa. At Ptolemy's order, the cortege was diverted southward, and by providing for the burial of his divine predecessor, first at Memphis and later in a tomb at Alexandria, Ptolemy thus set the stage for his own accession to the Throne of Horus.

Egypt was no melting pot, and under the Ptolemies the nation developed a curious split personality. In religion there was a symbolic synthesis, emphasized by the worship of a composite god, Serapis. The cult of Serapis combined features previously associated with that of Osiris, Lord of the Dead, and Apis, the sacred bull, but his appearance was distinctly Greek, with flowing locks and a Zeus-like scepter. The introduction of a new deity was, of course, a time-honored way of establishing political legitimacy in Egypt, but Serapis, worshiped almost entirely by Greeks,

The so-called "Alexander Sarcophagus" is thought to contain the body of King Abdalonymus of Sidon, who was installed on his throne by Alexander after the battle of Issus. The lid of the sarcophagus is shaped like the roof of a Classical temple. The sides depict scenes from Alexander's career, including (left) the lion hunt at Sidon.

Facing page, the dying Alexander. This Roman copy of a Hellenistic bust, now in the Uffizi Gallery, dramatizes the pathos of the conqueror's premature death.

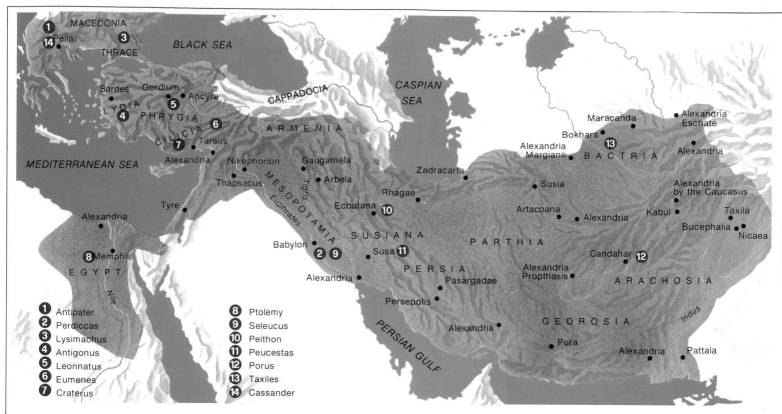

Map legend:

- ① Antipater
- ② Perdiccas
- ③ Lysimachus
- ④ Antigonus
- ⑤ Leonnatus
- ⑥ Eumenes
- ⑦ Craterus
- ⑧ Ptolemy
- ⑨ Seleucus
- ⑩ Peithon
- ⑪ Peucestas
- ⑫ Porus
- ⑬ Taxiles
- ⑭ Cassander

The kingdom after Alexander

After the death of Alexander in 323 B.C., the question of succession presented a difficult and perhaps insoluble problem. The two most obvious contenders were hardly fit to rule: Philip III Arrhidaeus, the bastard son of Philip II and therefore half-brother to Alexander, was mentally retarded, while Alexander's own son by his wife Roxane, named Alexander IV, was only a baby, born a few months after the great king's death.

In the absence of an acceptable successor, Alexander's most important generals made a compromise. The most influential of the group, the cavalry commander Perdiccas, who claimed to have received Alexander's signet ring, assumed the function of regent for the two kings on behalf of the

group. Their aim was to keep the empire united and to resist the separatist tendencies of other generals and satraps.

But the situation got out of control as these generals and satraps at once began to form coalitions among themselves in a series of constantly changing alliances. The result was a succession of internal wars that eventually broke up the empire. Perdiccas died in 321, followed by Antipater in 319. Henceforth, no regent was recognized by all the commanders, and the unity of the empire was in practice destroyed. By the year 315, the group of claimants had been narrowed to Antigonus the One-Eyed, who controlled Phrygia, Persia, and Media; Ptolemy, who held Egypt; Cassander, who ruled Macedonia and Thessaly; Seleucus, who controlled Babylonia; and Lysimachus, governor of Thrace.

The situation remained complex and fluid for the next twenty or so years, with

Below, coins of the successors: Lysimachus of Thrace (left); Philip III Arrhidaeus (center); and Demetrius Poliorcetes (right) in the first portrait of a European king coined during his lifetime. He wears bull's horns to emphasize his connection with Poseidon.

many sudden shifts of alliance. These years, however, saw an ascendancy of Antigonus the One-Eyed over the remaining rivals for the throne. With the help of his son Demetrius Poliorcetes, he ruled the largest slice of Alexander's empire. When he attempted to divide his enemies and conquer them separately, his opponents—though bitter rivals among themselves—managed to form alliances in time to stop him and save their respective kingdoms.

In 301, Antigonus was defeated and killed by a coalition of his rivals at the battle of Ipsus. His death signaled the end of the "imperial dream" of Alexander and his successors. It also marked the beginning of the three great kingdoms which, together with the politically divided yet still influential motherland of Greece, dominated the Hellenistic world: Egypt, which was to be ruled by Ptolemy and his succeeding Ptolemies and Cleopatras right down to the Roman conquest in 31 B.C.; Macedonia, ruled by Antigonus Gonatas, grandson of Antigonus the One-Eyed; and the Seleucid Empire, which at the time of the death of Seleucus I in 281 B.C. occupied an enormous tract of territory from the shores of the Mediterranean to the Indus.

Antigonus the One-Eyed

MACEDONIAN EMPIRE

Pella

The brilliant general Antigonus the One-Eyed emerged from the confusion immediately following Alexander's death with control of the Macedonian army in Asia and of the conqueror's treasury. Unfortunately for him, this powerful position—and his wish to make it even more powerful—also won him the collective enmity of the other successors: Ptolemy in Egypt, Seleucus in Babylon, Lysimachus in Thrace, and, in Macedonia, Antipater's son Cassander.

Antigonus went down fighting, dying at the age of eighty-one at the battle of Ipsus. His son Demetrius Poliorcetes claimed and, for a time, held the throne of Macedonia, but it was not until the reign of the old general's grandson Antigonus Gonatas (the "knock-kneed") that a semblance of stability was restored to the former domains of Philip II.

The Seleucids

When Alexander arranged for his commanders to wed daughters of the Persian nobility, Seleucus was not of sufficient rank to merit a member of the family of Darius III. He received instead a daughter of the rebel commander Spitamenes. While most of these diplomatic matches were dissolved after Alexander's death, Seleucus's marriage survived and became the foundation of the Seleucid dynasty.

Along with the other successors, Seleucus declared himself a king in the year 305 B.C. His enormous empire came to include all that the Persians had controlled in Asia, yet it quickly went into decline. The collapse of the Seleucid Empire demonstrated that a conquest as large as that of Alexander could never have held together without sufficient force exerted throughout the empire to maintain its cohesion, or a true unification of Greeks with the subject peoples of Asia. Both were lacking. Seleucus was forced to cede Alexander's conquered territory in India to the young Mauryan Empire. His descendants saw the rising of the Parthians erode their control over the eastern provinces of the empire and the revolt of the Jews in Palestine in 165 B.C. led by the Maccabees, who vehemently resented attempts at Hellenization.

Antiochus III, the Great (pictured here), campaigned vigorously in the East but failed to stem the growth of an independent Parthian Empire. His reign was in many ways a time of prosperity, but it also saw the beginning of the fall of the Seleucid Empire to Roman power. Antiochus was disastrously defeated by the Romans, and the treaty of Apamea in 188 forced him to relinquish Asia Minor and all claim to great power status. By the last century B.C., the Seleucid kingdom was reduced to Syria and to final decay, and in 64 B.C., it became the Roman province of Syria.

Pergamon

Antioch

Euphrates

Tigris

Ecbatana

SELEUCID EMPIRE

Babylon

Persepolis

Indus

Nile

Ptolemy

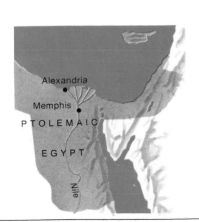

Alexandria

Memphis

PTOLEMAIC

EGYPT

Nile

Ptolemy had been close to Alexander for most of his life, and he was one of a few friends who shared the prince's exile from the court of Philip II. After the conqueror's death, Ptolemy made sure that their symbolic association would continue. His claim that Alexander had asked to be buried at Siwa may have been true, but it also served as a pretext to snatch Alexander's body and bury it in Alexandria, the new capital city. This shrewd act provided him with insurance for his claim to the Throne of Horus in Egypt.

Ptolemy eventually declared himself ruler of Egypt in his own right. In 280 B.C., he became, posthumously, a god. The deification, ordered by his son Ptolemy II Philadelphus to shore up his own claims to dynastic legitimacy, was widely imitated throughout the Hellenistic world.

never eclipsed the established gods, whose temples the Ptolemies continued to maintain.

Religion aside, contact between the cultures of conquerors and conquered was minimal. The Nile's new rulers wore the traditional double crown and uraeus symbol of the ancient pharaohs, but in reality only a very small number of native-born Egyptians held office in their governments. The great accomplishment of the early Ptolemies rested on their skill at putting Egypt on a sound business basis. They established two currencies—bronze for use at home, gold and silver for international commerce. The Ptolemies also introduced a new strain of wheat more suitable for export and encouraged the cultivation of crops, such as olives, which were in demand throughout the Mediterranean. But as had been the case even before Alexander's conquest, foreign trade was largely in the hands of the foreign born.

Like the new upper class of Greeks and other Hellenized subjects who ran their kingdom, the Ptolemies drank wine instead of beer and spoke Greek. But oddly enough, they were quick to adopt one Egyptian custom, that of brother-sister marriages. Ptolemy II Philadelphus set the pattern by marrying his formidable sister Arsinoë, and the last scion of the dynasty, Cleopatra VII, had been married to two of her half-brothers before she caught the attention of Julius Caesar.

The spiritual split between Hellenic and Egyptian culture was embodied in a geographic division between the countryside and the capital. Alexandria, the new capital of Hellenic civilization, was a large and truly international city, with over three hundred thousand inhabitants from all over the Mediterranean world. *Koine,* a modified form of the Attic dialect adopted by the Macedonians, was the language of all educated Alexandrians, about half of whom came from mainland Greece, the Greek islands, or Macedonia. There was also a large Jewish community, whose relationship to the ruling Greeks was am-

The Ptolemies gave Egypt its first system of currency (left). Bronze coins were used within the country while precious metals were reserved for foreign transactions. Ptolemy I (top) appears on the obverse of a gold octadrachma minted between 246 and 221 B.C.; center, the Greco-Egyptian god Zeus-Amon; bottom, the cornucopia symbol of the Ptolemies.

Facing page, Kom Ombo on the eastern bank of the Nile in Upper Egypt, near Aswan. This region was sacred to Horus and Sobek.

bivalent. On the one hand, Alexandria was the home of assimilationist philosophers like the first-century A.D. Philo, who combined Hebrew monotheism with the teachings of Plato. ("Plato philosophized; Philo platonizes," said the wags.) On the other hand, Alexandria may well have been the birthplace of anti-Semitism. This attitude was already evident in Manetho, who was the first to set down the dynastic chronology of the pharaohs. He actually made the case that the Hebrews of the Exodus were merely a colony of lepers expelled from Egypt.

As traditional Egypt had the Great Pyramids of Giza, Alexandria boasted of the Pharos lighthouse, four hundred feet tall and topped by a polished steel mirror said to be visible to ships thirty miles away. Built by Sostratus of Cnidus during the reign of Ptolemy II, it symbolized commercial Alexandria. The

Mouseion (Museum) was the symbol of the city's intellectual pre-eminence. This "temple of the muses" was not a museum in the modern sense, but a center for research. In addition to a world-renowned library, the Ptolemies also built a zoo and a botanical garden. Despots that they were, the Ptolemies were generous in their support of intellectuals; scholars were exempt from taxes and often enjoyed living allowances from the state, a situation succinctly summed up by one Ctesibius who, when asked what philosophy had given him, answered simply, "free meals."

Though participation in a community where the wisdom of many cultures intermingled was exciting, creative artists could no longer address their work to a homogeneous audience with a common system of belief. An inevitable result was the beginning of a distinction between "highbrow" and "lowbrow" art.

The librarians, bibliographers, and textual scholars of the Mouseion were responsible for preserving many literary masterpieces of Classical Greece, but this emphasis on scholarship is usually counted against Alexandrian writers, whose works tend to be highly stylized and laced with literary and historical allusions. Yet they initiated a number of developments that still have great appeal. For one, romantic love was now considered a worthy theme for serious writing. Above all, Hellenistic writers displayed a zest for particulars, filling their works with close and often lively descriptions of characters, dialects, and scenes.

A passion for observation and cataloguing led to dramatic results in science. Euclid, the father of geometry, is probably the best-remembered Alexandrian mathematician, but experimental scientists like Hipparchus of Nicaea and Eratosthenes of Cyrene were more typical. The former produced a star catalogue, describing more than eight hundred heavenly bodies. The latter calculated the circumference of the earth by taking measurements at Alexandria and at Aswan of the angles of shadows cast by the midsummer sun at noon, arriving at a solution that erred by only fifty miles, a remarkable achievement even though it was partly the result of errors that canceled each other out.

Above all, Alexandria was a mecca for physicians,

who came to Egypt less because of the country's traditional excellence in medical practice than because of the ready supply of corpses for dissection. Herophilus reasserted that the brain was the seat of thought and the center of the nervous system. Most Alexandrian doctors, however, favored the Empirical school, which emphasized observation and proven cures. In the long run, the Empiricists' neglect of theory was counterproductive, but their stress on clinical practice did inject a refreshing element of common sense into a field that was at the time rife with the most irrelevant theorizing. "If theory produced doctors," wrote one Empiricist, "then philosophers would be the best doctors; as it is, they have words to spare, but no knowledge of healing."

These developments in Alexandria were by no means isolated from the rest of the Hellenistic world. The city's major rival for intellectual leadership was Pergamon in Asia Minor, which enjoyed political independence from 263 until 133 B.C., when its last king deeded his domains to Rome. The competition of Pergamon's famous library was so keenly felt in Alexandria that Ptolemy V imposed an embargo on papyrus exports, which led the Pergamenes to invent parchment. But it was to warfare that most of Pergamon's energies were devoted as they were forced to fight off the Galatians or Gauls. This memorable struggle is portrayed in the city's most important monument, the Altar of Zeus as an epic battle between gods and giants.

Each in its own way, Pergamon and Alexandria were exceptional; the real testing ground for Alexander's faith in the *polis* as the bearer of Greek civilization came in Asia. After Alexander's death, practical control over the former Persian Empire had been divided among a number of Macedonian-born satraps who were soon fighting among themselves for dominance. In the series of battles and intrigues that followed, the titular monarchs were stripped of their power and eventually murdered. The man to emerge victorious from these struggles was Seleucus, Alexander's former lieutenant.

The empire founded by Seleucus was notably unstable, plagued by native rebellions in its more distant provinces, dynastic wars at its center, and a running contest with the Ptolemies for control of Pales-

Above center, a relief from the temple of Hathor at Dandarah on the left bank of the Nile in Upper Egypt and (immediately right) a Greco-Roman stele of gray granite now in the Cairo Museum. Despite the use of traditional Egyptian iconography, Greek influence is evident, especially in the modeling of human figures.

142

A Ptolemaic period mural (above) shows a woman in a Greek-style draped garment flanked by Egyptian divinities. Below, evidence of the once-beautiful "Sacred Lake" of the Dandarah temple.

Left, Ptolemy V Epiphanes, whose reign was marred by widespread revolt.

They boasted Greek *gymnasia* and sometimes theaters, and they worshiped Greek gods.

The gymnasium had long ceased to be merely a center for physical exercise. Combining the functions of a club and a school, it played a primary role in the Greek concept of educating the whole man—a philosophy quite different from the scribal traditions of the East, where literacy in itself was highly valued. The first citizens of the new Asian cities were Greek and Macedonian, but in contrast to Egypt, where the gymnasia remained the exclusive clubs of the conquerors, there was considerable assimilation of the native population. For the upper classes, at least, the acquisition of Greek language and culture could be the passport to full participation in local government. Land-owning aristocrats were among the first to be Hellenized; and since Greek rule was generally associated with commercial expansion, Hellenization was also attractive to wealthy urbanites.

For the masses, who soon found themselves separated from their rulers by barriers of language and culture, Hellenistic civilization offered considerably less. What proportion of the population was actually enslaved is debatable, but there is little question that the laboring classes, whether slave or free, had a difficult life. In the cities, some people were able to move

tine and Phoenicia. The Seleucid kings were almost constantly at war, but in spite of these troubles, their policy of Hellenizing Asia's cities and towns was remarkably successful. The important trade routes, from Asia Minor and Palestine all the way to the Oxus River, were dominated by towns with Hellenic names. As many as thirty-four cities had been founded by Alexander himself, but Seleucus and his descendants continued to build, establishing at least nine Seleucias and sixteen Antiochs. These towns controlled their own affairs through institutions borrowed from the traditions of the Greek city-state.

The temple of Isis at Philae (left), an island near the Nile's First Cataract, was an important cult center through Roman times. In this century, the temple was threatened by flooding created by the Aswan High Dam until an international rescue crew painstakingly moved the entire structure to a safe location a hundred feet above the old valley floor.

Below, the portrait of a middle-aged priest, Hor-Si-Hor. He is represented with Greek features, hair style, and costume in a distinctively Egyptian pose. This papyrus (right) of 170 B.C. records the proceedings of a civil law-suit over property, fought between the children of a first and a second marriage.

into the new middle class of businessmen, functionaries, and administrators, but for the most part the poor were as poor as ever. And though the bureaucracy of the Seleucids never rivaled that developed by the Ptolemies, the primary representative of Hellenization to the rural masses must surely have been the tax or rent collector.

The role of mercenaries in this new society was crucial. Recruited from Macedonia, the Greek islands, and the poorest regions of the mainland, they soon found themselves serving far from home, where the climate was uncongenial and the population exotic. In the beginning, Hellenistic monarchs did everything possible to induce the mercenaries to stay in their kingdoms and to settle there for good. During the third century B.C., mercenaries typically enjoyed high pay and special privileges. Often, they were given grants of land to encourage them to marry and establish new roots. These grants, or *cleruchies*, were originally supposed to revert to the crown on the soldier's death, but in many places tenure became hereditary. Nevertheless, the mercenaries' security was closely tied to that of the kingdoms they served, and during the long decline of the empire, their pay was often cut off. By the second century B.C., the lot of the mercenary was sometimes hardly distinguishable

Flax monopoly

Although a beautiful Greek legend attributes the invention of linen thread to a Lydian girl called Arachne, it is most likely that it was the ancient Nile dwellers who first spun and wove the flax plant. Since the age of the Old Kingdom, the Egyptians had used the cloth for sacred purposes, wrapping mummies in bandages made of the finest linen. Presumably the linen industry spread to countries of the East, but for most of the ancient peoples of the Mediterranean, linen remained a rare and costly import. Until the age of Pericles, the Greeks dressed uniformly in wool, only a few wealthy people being able to afford a tunic of cool linen. Even in Rome, linen garments were an exotic luxury, looked on with suspicion by traditionalists.

It was only during the Roman Empire that linen cloth came to be as widely used as wool. This was thanks to Hellenistic Egypt. Under the Ptolemies, and later as a province, Egypt became so adept at working linen that the Egyptians practically had a world monopoly, in production as well as in trade.

We learn how flax was worked from the *Natural History* of Pliny the Elder. The plants were tied in bundles and dried in the sun, then soaked in water and dried once more. When fully dry, they were beaten with special hammers. The husks were used as wicks for oil lamps, while the fine inner fibers were combed, bleached, spun, and woven on special looms. At this point the state intervened, for its omnipresent officials kept a rigid control on production. All the looms were officially registered, and the weavers had to first supply the state—and at prices fixed by the government. Then came the temples, which had many uses for linen. Finally, the remainder belonged to the weaver, for his own use or for sale. Under this system, half free trade and half state controlled, the linen industry prospered for centuries, much to the benefit of the Egyptian economy.

Right, four stages in the manufacture of linen: from raw flax (below left), to the fiber in rough plaits (below right) and in skeins (above right), and finally after spinning and weaving, to long strips stored in rolls (above left).

from that of the peasant.

While the mercenaries were often attracted to local cults and mystery religions, even in bad times they remained surprisingly devoted to Hellenic culture. In the Greco-Bactrian and Greco-Indian kingdoms of the East, where the descendants of Alexander's soldiers and the Seleucids constituted a minority of the population, Greek institutions survived until the second—and in some cases the first—century B.C. Artifacts produced in Syria and Alexandria have been discovered at Begram, near modern Kabul, and King Menander, almost certainly a convert to Buddhism, continued to issue coins bearing a typically Macedonian representation of Athena.

Although Hellenization took different forms in different countries, it was generally avidly embraced by the upper classes. There was at least one important exception: Judaea. As monotheists, the Jews faced a unique problem in accommodating to the polis system. To participate in the life of the polis, a citizen not only had to know Greek but also had to worship the official gods of the civic cult. For most, this was a formality; for a Jew, it meant repudiation of the Mosaic law. (A more mundane but still significant problem was that a Jew could not attend the gymnasium, where nudity was practiced, without revealing his circumcised state.)

When the Seleucids wrested the territory of Judaea from the Ptolemies, Antiochus III continued the Egyptian policy of allowing the Jews to live "accord-

Ptolemy VIII Euergetes appears at Kom Ombo in the company of Re-Harakhte and Sobek (left). The reign of Ptolemy VIII was marked by continual dynastic struggles that contributed to the decline of the Egyptian state, which was already weakened politically though still vigorous as a center of Hellenistic culture.

Weights and measures

The Egyptians were the first people to devise a properly organized system of weights and measures. The measure of length was the "cubit" (from the Latin word for elbow), which more or less corresponded to the length of the human forearm from the tip of the middle finger to the elbow. The cubit was subdivided into twenty-eight "fingers," and four of these made a "span."

The finger could be subdivided into smaller units by a somewhat complicated method: On a cubit rule the fourteenth finger was divided into sixteen equal parts, the next into fifteen, and so on up to the twenty-eighth, which was divided into two. With this system, any length could be measured with precision.

For measuring weights, the Egyptians used what might be called a decimal system. The basic unit was the "kite"; ten kites made a "deben," and ten debens made a "sep." The actual weights were either stones or pieces of metal in various shapes, often representing animals. There are, in fact, records of over 3,400 varieties of animal-shaped weights used by the ancient Egyptians.

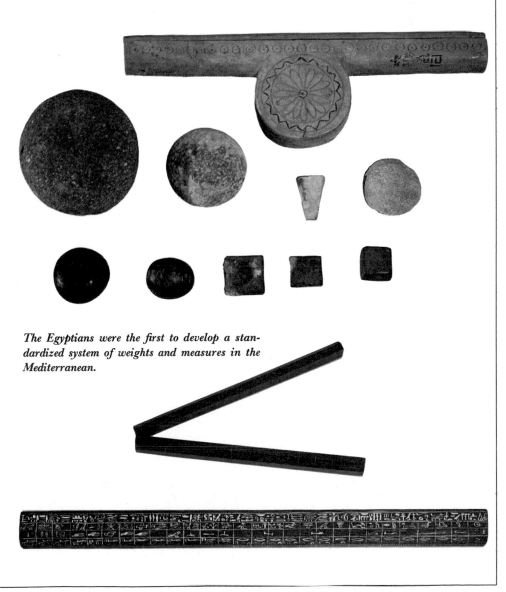

The Egyptians were the first to develop a standardized system of weights and measures in the Mediterranean.

Encounter with Rome

The British Classicist Gilbert Murray once wrote that Hellenistic society had suffered from a "failure of nerve." The phrase aptly captures the mood of anxiety and rootlessness that pervaded the Hellenistic kingdoms after Alexander's death. Yet even in the shadow of the Roman takeover, the Hellenistic world continued to produce brilliant and energetic individuals. Archimedes, best known for having discovered the principles of specific gravity and buoyancy while meditating in his bathtub, was a creative mathematical theorist. Though he set little value on his ingenious mechanical inventions, he was pressed into designing war engines for his patron, Heiro, king of Syracuse, who used them successfully to resist the Roman siege for three years.

A more celebrated, and still more misunderstood, representative of Hellenism was Cleopatra VII. As the last heir to the throne whose power and effectiveness had been declining for two centuries, Cleopatra recognized that the future of the Mediterranean lay with Rome and that her personal charm was her greatest political asset. Cleopatra was neither the striking beauty nor the assimilated Egyptian princess pictured in so many historical romances. She could speak Egyptian, an ability the earlier Ptolemies would have scorned, but her mastery of philosophy, business, and the art of intrigue brought her to the attention of Caesar and then of Mark Antony. Had Fortune been with Cleopatra, Rome's emperors might have descended from a Macedonian queen.

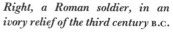

Right, a Roman soldier, in an ivory relief of the third century B.C.

Below, the siege of Syracuse, commemorated on a Roman coin of the republican period. The Syracusan king Hieronymus was an ally of Rome's mortal enemy, Carthage.

Archimedes (above) applied his theoretical knowledge of mathematics and mechanics to the practical problem of designing machines for defending Syracuse. He conceived the idea of using mirrors to concentrate the sun's rays on the enemy's ships and set them on fire.

Pompey's Pillar (left) rises near the former site of the Serapeum, the Ptolemies' temple to their syncretistic god, Serapis. Few monuments of Hellenistic Alexandria survived the Arab conquest of the seventh century A.D. The pillar, despite its legendary associations with Pompey, dates from the reign of Diocletian (third century A.D.).

Above, an idealized portrait of Cleopatra VII, from the Cherchell Museum, Algiers.

Below, Julius Caesar, the alleged father of Cleopatra's son Caesarion, who reigned briefly as Ptolemy XVI.

ing to their ancestral laws." Conflict did not begin in earnest until the reign of Antiochus IV, when the High Priest Joshua, better known by his Hellenized name of Jason, was given the right to make Jerusalem a polis and to build a gymnasium near the hill of Zion. This move exacerbated a long-standing division between the Hellenized Jews, mostly wealthy aristocrats, and those who adhered to the religious laws. When factional squabbles broke out, Antiochus suspected—with some justice—that the issue was being used as an excuse to solicit the return of the Ptolemies. In reaction, he issued an edict in 167 B.C. that forbade observance of the Sabbath and converted the temple of Jerusalem into a shrine of Zeus-Olympus. These acts of persecution brought on the guerrilla wars of the Maccabees.

Judas Maccabaeus retook Jerusalem and purified the temple in 165 B.C., but the passions ignited by Antiochus IV never completely died down. Politically, they culminated in the establishment of a separate Jewish kingdom, which lasted until the time of Herod. Spiritually, they led to the rise of competing sects, each one searching for a new balance between the letter and the spirit of the law, and to a growing longing for the Messiah.

For the Seleucid king, meanwhile, the plundering of the temple in Jerusalem had been small compen-

sation for the losses he was suffering at the hands of the Roman Empire. As further consolation for his deteriorating situation, Antiochus staged a vain show of glory, celebrating his return from Judaea and Egypt with a grand festival of games and pageantry. The event was held near the Seleucid capital of Antioch-on-the-Orontes, and a contemporary account by the historian Polybius helps to explain why the Antiochians were famed for their love of luxury and good living. "The vast quantity of images is impossible to enumerate," Polybius wrote. "All . . . were carried along, some gilded, others draped in garments embroidered with gold, and they were all accompanied by representations executed in precious metals of the myths relating to them as traditionally narrated. . . .The slaves of one of the royal 'friends,' Dionysis, the private secretary, marched along carry-

ing articles of silver plate none of them weighing less than a thousand drachmas. . . . Next there were about two hundred women sprinkling the crowd with perfumes from golden urns. . . ." Finally, Polybius noted that "for banqueting there were sometimes a thousand tables laid and sometimes fifteen hundred, all furnished with the most costly viands."

Splendid as it was, the pageantry was but a feeble attempt on the part of Antiochus to forget his recent humiliation at the hands of Rome. Having finally won a decisive victory in Egypt, he watched impotently in 168 B.C. as Rome declared itself the "protec-

tor" of the Ptolemies. The Roman Senate sent an envoy, Popillius Laenas, to demand Antiochus's withdrawal from Egyptian territory. It is said that, when Antiochus requested time to consider his answer, Laenas drew a circle around the emperor's feet and demanded that he respond before he stepped beyond its perimeter. Antiochus could only agree. Faced by challenges from the east and rebellions within their own borders, the kings of Antioch now watched both Egypt and Macedon slip within the Roman orbit.

For the Macedonians, the year 168 B.C. had also

Above, Antiochus III the Great. He drove the Ptolemies from Phoenicia and reigned during the most glorious era of the Seleucid Empire. His reign also marked the Seleucids' first clash with the rising power of Rome.

Above right, a fragment of a bronze portrait of Antiochus IV, the flamboyant son and successor to Antiochus the Great. Right, a signet ring bearing the seal of Seleucus I.

been one of defeat: King Perseus lost a decisive encounter with the Romans at the battle of Pydna. The fall of Macedonia was not really surprising, for, despite the efforts of several able kings, Fortune had not been kind to Philip II's dream of a unified Greece under Macedonian direction. In the struggles for power that followed Alexander's death, Macedon suffered the most. And while Macedonians abroad lived in cosmopolitan Alexandria and the luxury-loving Antioch, their homeland remained provincial. Not until 276 B.C., when Antigonus Gonatas finally established himself at Pella and began inviting Greek philosophers, poets, and historians to his court, did Macedon recapture some of the cultural gloss that had been missing since the days of Philip II.

Antigonus Gonatas made a promising beginning, but there was no way that he could turn the clock back a hundred years. Greece itself was in decline; its best and most energetic citizens had emigrated to populate the new cities of Asia; and the once-proud cities of Hellas experienced declining production, unplowed fields, and demoralizing poverty. Athens was for a time an exception to the confused state of the Greek economy, but by 261, even Athens had aban-

Demetrius I Soter (above) spent his early years as a hostage in Rome but returned to Antioch to drive his cousin Antiochus V from the throne. His twelve-year reign was a troubled one, marred by the continuing Maccabean revolt in Judaea, dissension at home, and clashes with Pergamon. In 150 B.C., he was killed in a battle against the Pergamene-supported pretender, Alexander Balas.

The head of a Seleucid statuette (left), found at Avaresh near Teheran, recalls the style of the so-called Tanagra figures, manufactured in Greece.

Pergamon

Pergamon, one of the chief centers of Hellenistic civilization, was an ancient fortress city magnificently situated astride a steep hill that had been known in Alexander's lifetime as a nesting ground for eagles. According to legend, Pergamon—now Bergama in western Turkey—was founded by the demi-god Telephus, but it can be said to have been refounded by the Attalid dynasty.

The Attalids employed Hellenistic architects to sculpt the great hillside and erect the chief buildings on terraces. In the lower town, on three parallel terraces, were the *agora* (marketplace), the gymnasium, a theater built into the hillside, and the library, second only to that of Alexandria. Halfway up the hill was the enclosure sacred to Hera and the sanctuary of Demeter. At the top, on the acropolis, stood the royal palace.

Also at the summit was one of the Seven Wonders of the Ancient World, the massive Altar of Zeus and Athena built in the reign of the Attalid ruler Eumenes II. The altar, which attracted the talents of artists from all over the Hellenistic world, bore a continuous frieze in high relief, depicting the war of the gods and the giants. On its exalted hilltop site, the monument commemorates the efforts of the Attalid monarchs to defeat the hordes of Gauls who had invaded Asia Minor.

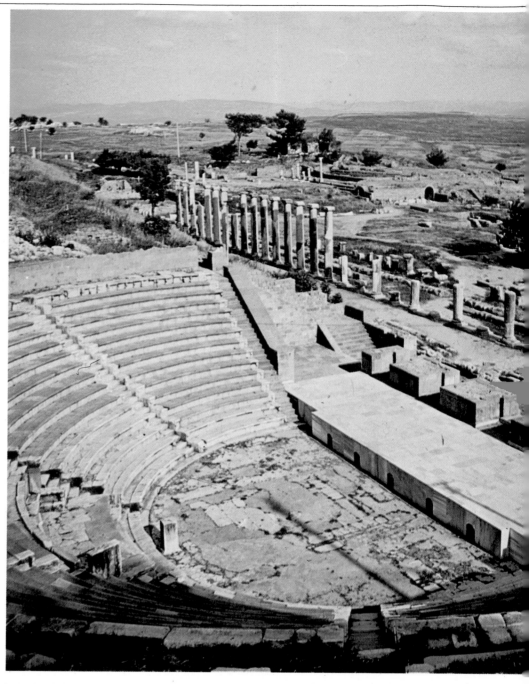

Above right, the restored theater of Pergamon, and near right, the ruins of a Pergamene-colonnaded street.

Pergamon's library (above) rivaled that of Alexandria and was said to contain two hundred thousand volumes.

Below center, a temple dedicated to Telesphorus, son of Aesculapius. Below right, a sacred spring whose waters were believed to have curative powers.

Above, a beaten gold wreath from Pergamon.

Below right, a coin bearing the portrait of Philetaeros, founder of the Attalid dynasty.

by refraining from desires not easily satisfied. In practice, this meant leading an austere and simple life. Epicurus's doctrines had enormous appeal to Hellenes, who found themselves surrounded by foreign cults and customs. Their appeal was especially strong in the East where they attracted influential followers.

In Athens, some people felt Epicurus did not go far

doned its silver coinage. Heraclides the physician made a telling summary of the city's fortunes when he remarked that Athens was still the most delightful place in the world—provided one brought one's own food.

What Athens did have, much to the envy of Gonatas, were philosophers. From 307 B.C. on, the city was home to the school of Epicurus, a controversial thinker whose ideas reflected the uncertainties and rootlessness that pervaded Hellenistic society. Epicurus advised his followers to "avoid the public eye," a rule he followed by living in semi-retirement, teaching his disciples from the privacy of his own garden. According to Epicurus, pleasure was the only worthwhile object of life; but rather than a wholehearted pursuit of luxury, he counseled minimizing the pain inevitable in life, avoiding disappointment

enough. The Cynics, or "Dog Philosophers" as they were called, anticipated the reverse of fate by divesting themselves of their property in advance. Many became wandering mendicants, haranguing strangers on street corners or entering houses unannounced to preach to the inhabitants. Bion of Borysthenes, a rhetorician who popularized the ideas of the more serious Cynics, summed up this philosophical attitude by noting that "Fortune is like a dramatist who designs a number of parts. . . . What the good man has to do is to play well any part for which Fortune casts him."

Oddly enough, it was a pupil of Crates, the best-known Cynic of the time, who made Fortune seem less threatening once again. Zeno of Cyprus, who arrived in Athens in about 336 B.C., agreed with the goal of *autarky,* or self-sufficiency. For him, unlike Epicurus, virtue and not pleasure was the path to this end. Zeno's school of Stoicism restored the concepts of universal order and eternal law. He taught that history was cyclic and that, while individuals could only accept their allotted role in life, at least they were governed by destiny rather than chance. This philosophy had obvious appeal for an activist, ambitious ruler like Gonatas, and he particularly wanted the Stoic to grace his court at Pella. Zeno replied by sending one of his pupils to tutor the Macedonian crown prince, pleading that he was too old to make the journey himself.

Zeno might just as well have said that it was too late. The situation in the western Mediterranean was

Fatally wounded, the Dying Gaul (below) has dropped his battle trumpet and is preparing to drag himself from the field. This Roman copy of a figure from a monument not only celebrates Attalus I's victory over the Gauls (Galatians), but also draws inspiration from the courage of the defeated.

Left, Antiochus VII as Perseus. Combining a faithful representation of Antiochus's face with an idealized body in the Classical mode, this bronze statuette is a curious blend of aesthetic traditions. Antiochus VII was the son of Cleopatra Thea, pictured (above) with her husband, Alexander Balas.

far less stable than it had been a century before, a lesson Gonatas learned only two years later, in 274 B.C., when he was briefly deposed by the ambitious King Pyrrhus of Epirus, a member of the family that had produced Alexander's mother, Olympias. Gonatas managed to defeat and kill Pyrrhus, thereby regaining control of Macedon, but challenges to Macedonian supremacy came from powerful outside enemies. The first was Egypt, where Ptolemy II had married his sister Arsinoë, who happened to be the widow of two of the now-deceased pretenders to the Macedonian throne. Ptolemy II and his son kept up their interest in Greek politics by inciting anti-Macedonian policies in Athens, Sparta, and elsewhere in Greece until 222 B.C., when Sparta was crushed by the Macedonians and became subject to their control. The Ptolemies henceforth had their own troubles and kept out of Greek affairs. A year later a new king, seventeen-year-old Philip V, came to the throne in Pella. Philip was a talented general and an energetic politician who sparked memories of Alexander the Great, yet there was little he could do to unite the factional Hellenes against the rising tide of Rome. Philip fought two wars with Rome. The first, which

ΤΗΝΛΑΟCΙ Κ I Υ C Ι Π
ΤΑΥ ΤΗ ΙΕΡΟΥ ΑΦΛΑ
ΛΕΓΟΜΕΝΟΥ ΟCΟΥ
ΤΗC ΑΝΑΘ ΛΛΩΜΗC
ΕΥΦΡΑΤΟΥ ΑΝΕΟΗΚΕΝ
ΑΥ ΛΔΙΑΒΟC
ΖΑΒΔΙΒΩΛΟΥ ΤΟΥ
CΗΛΛΟΙ ΕΥΧΗΝ
ΥΠΕΡΤΗC
CΩΤΗΡΙ
ΑΥΤΟΥ
ΚΑΙΤΕ Κ Ν Ω
ΚΑΙΤΟΠΑΤ C
ΤΟ ΙΚΟΥ

Left, the Semitic god Aphlad, honored on a Hellenistic relief from Dura-Europos, on the Euphrates in Mesopotamia. The worship of indigenous gods continued in many localities.

Hellenistic art and the grotesque

Bent on exploring the extremes of the human condition, Hellenistic artists included scenes of violence, ugliness, and drunkenness in their works. This attraction to the earthier, even grotesque, side of human nature was one aspect of the cosmopolitan spirit of the age. Artists traveled widely, and they were exposed to a great variety of cultures and people. They were also influenced by growing scholarly interest in biography and psychology.

As the Hellenistic scientist was interested in observing and explaining all natural phenomena, however seemingly insignificant, so the Hellenistic artist was intrigued by deformed dwarfs, ancient hags, and wretched beggars—as well as the traditional beautiful young men and spotless maidens. Although there are traces of caricature or satire in the great works of the age of Pericles, Greek artists were almost exclusively concerned with achieving an ideal of beauty in their art. The later Hellenistic artists broadened the range of acceptable subject matter and represented man as he is, not as an ideal.

Declining faith in the Olympian gods also played a part in the freedom of the Hellenistic sculptor, whose work was no longer required to have a religious purpose. But at the same time, the tendency to treat temples as art galleries rather than as places of worship fostered an intense if somewhat self-conscious admiration for the Classical past. For the first time in history, art collecting became a popular and highly competitive pastime. A superior copy of an acknowledged masterpiece was in itself a work of art that might fetch a high price, but there was also an international market for reproductions, mass-produced in bronze or terra cotta.

Below left, a drunken old woman cradling a wine jug in her arms. The detail, which is from a Roman copy of an original by Myron of Pergamon, is one of many variations on the popular theme of "the old derelict."

Below right, the muse Polyhymnia. Her pose, with a finger under the chin, is meant to suggest a visionary trance.

Below, a satyr and nymph. A vogue for complex compositions, especially involving violent and passionate human entanglements, gave Hellenistic sculptors a chance to demonstrate their technical virtuosity.

Right, another satyr, from the so-called "Invitation to the Dance." The cymbals in the satyr's hands were added during a faulty restoration.

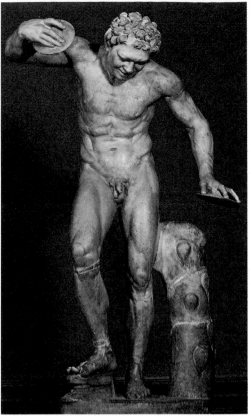

The old man (below), holding an empty wine cup, rests on the lid of a sarcophagus.

Gold work

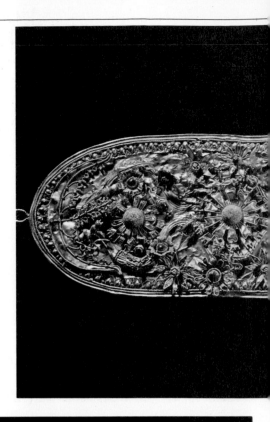

Contrary to the popular image of classical serenity and simplicity, the Greeks always loved decoration, and their goldsmiths excelled at creating such finely crafted objects as victory crowns and gold-leaf decoration for statuary. What limited these Classical craftsmen was not a lack of skill, but the scarcity of gold.

With the capture of the Persian treasury, Greece and Macedonia were flooded with gold. Though the sudden influx of wealth had a disastrous effect on the economy, touching off rampant inflation, it also inspired a dramatic increase in the production of gold jewelry, much of it designed to suit the tastes of the Persian ladies in Alexander's court.

Persian-inspired jewelry tended to be richer and heavier than that favored in earlier times by the Greeks, though the love of filigree and floral elaboration—including tendrils, scrolls, and palmettos—survived into Hellenistic times. Nevertheless, the virtuoso style inspired by the craftsman's need to display a maximum of skill with a minimum of raw material gradually lost favor as the use of precious and semi-precious stones became more predominant. By the second century B.C., the gold work itself commonly assumed a humble position, often functioning as little more than a setting for the stones.

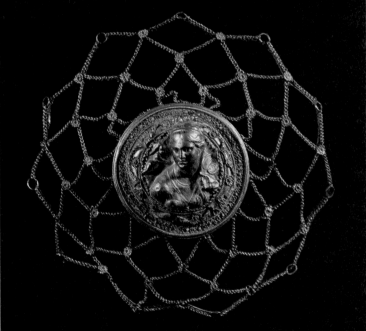

Some of the splendid articles of jewelry found in Thessaly in 1929 include: a golden crown with a laurel-leaf pattern (above), which was fairly common at Hellenistic courts; a medallion with a bust of the goddess Artemis wearing the chiton and a wild animal's skin fastened on the left shoulder (above right); a woman's diadem with a central medallion and pendants (right). The main difference between these objects and those of Thracian and Scythian workmanship is the almost complete absence of animal representations.

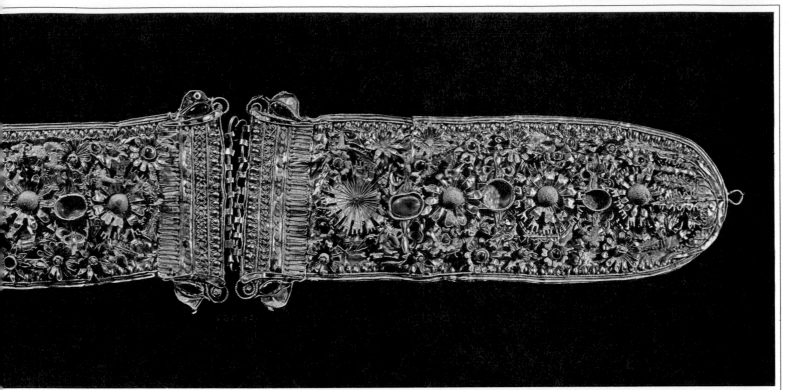

Other artworks from the treasure recovered at Thessaly are now in the Elena Stathatos Collection: a broad and elaborately decorated golden belt (above); a bracelet in the form of a snake and a series of pendant earrings (right); a woman's golden diadem with pendants at the sides (below); and a long, narrow belt with an intricately worked clasp (below right).

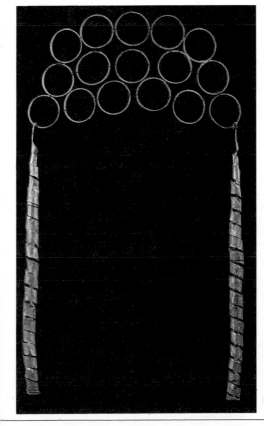

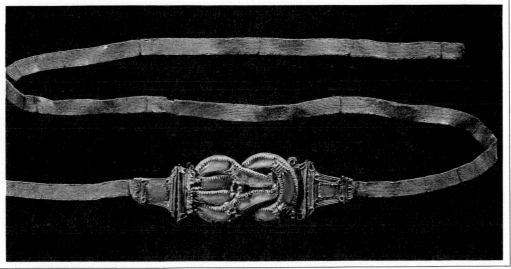

Greek inscription on the funeral slab:
ΔΙΟΝΥΣΙΟΥ ΤΟΥ ΓΑΜΜΕΝΟΥ ΔΙΟΝΥΣΙΟΥ ΘΕΟΚΡΙΤΟΥ ΤΟ
ΡΑΝΑΣΙΟΝΟΣ ΤΟΥΝΟΥΜΗΝΙΟΥ ΤΥΡΑΝΧΙΟΥ ΒΑΚΧΟΥ

Above, a banquet scene from a Hellenistic funeral slab at Erdek, Turkey.

was provoked by Philip's alliance with Carthage, drew Roman forces into Greece for the first time. The second, which began just a few years after the end of the first in 205, was launched by the Romans to crush Philip before he could mobilize against Rome. Rome succeeded, and Philip was forced to become an ally of Rome and to withdraw his forces from Greece. After the defeat of Sparta, the Roman general Titus Quinctius Flamininus grandly announced the withdrawal of all Roman forces from Greece as well, presenting himself as the "liberator" of Greece.

Upheavals eventually forced the Romans to return to the Greek mainland, and Macedonia was destroyed in a third war in 168. In that year Rome declared itself the "protector" of the defeated and demoralized Ptolemies, preventing the Seleucid king Antiochus IV from capitalizing on his military victories in Egypt. The Seleucid kingdom was shrinking, and the rise of the Maccabees, encouraged by Rome, further weakened the state whose power was effectively finished with the death of Antiochus in 163. The last Attalid king, Attalos III, may have foreseen the inevitable; in 133, he left his kingdom in his will to the Roman people. The following century was one long series of coups, rebellions, wars, and economic disasters. Even Nature seemed to conspire against the remnants of Hellenistic power. In 148 B.C., and again in 130 B.C., Antioch was nearly destroyed by numerous earthquakes.

By the middle of the first century B.C., Rome had inherited the remains of Alexander's empire. With it, the Romans adopted the philosophy of the Stoics, which gave them the moral and political justification for their own imperial age. No doubt the Aristotelians would have regarded this turn of events as just one more proof of the violent and fickle nature of Fortune, but later generations have better appreciated the significance of Alexander the Great's meteoric career

Below, a Tanagra statuette, named after the city in Boeotia. These figurines, manufactured by the thousands, were sold throughout the Hellenistic world. Fashioned from bronze, wood, stone, or more typically, from terra cotta, the statuettes were intended for use in tombs and sanctuaries, as well as on private altars.

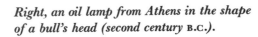

Above, Aphrodite and Eros, portrayed on a bronze mirror cover of the late fourth century B.C. The rather insipid style is derived from Attic vase painting.

Right, an oil lamp from Athens in the shape of a bull's head (second century B.C.).

and of the quarrelsome and anxiety-ridden kingdoms of his successors.

By proclaiming himself divine, Alexander created a precedent that was imitated, not just by his direct heirs, but by the Roman emperors as well. He thus gave the West a new justification for absolutism—as well as a personal example that made ruthless, and apparently motiveless, conquest seem noble and even civilized.

Yet Alexander's conquests also set the stage for the emergence of Western culture as we know it. It was through Hellenistic society that Greek art, literature, and philosophy came to influence the Romans and, eventually, all of Europe. Less directly, through the translation of the Hebrew Scriptures into Greek and the events that inspired the revolt of the Maccabees, Hellenization prepared the way for Judaism's profound impact on the Roman world. Above all, by creating, however briefly, a unified empire that transcended national boundaries and local cults, Alexander encouraged an entirely new perception of the scale of world civilization. Without his vision, the reign of Roman law and the spread of Christianity would have been impossible. W. W. Tarn, Alex-

ander's staunchest twentieth-century admirer, grandly described this new outlook: "Above all," he wrote, "Alexander inspired Zeno's vision of a world in which all men should be members of one another, citizens of one State without distinction of race or institutions, subject only to and in harmony with the Common Law immanent in the Universe."

Above left, a relief personifying Helicon, the Boeotian mountain sacred to the muses and to Apollo. Ganymede (below left) was a Trojan youth whose beauty so attracted Zeus that he abducted him to perform as cupbearer for the Olympian gods.

Facing page, the "Winged Victory of Samothrace." Her triumphant pose and rich, sensuous draperies capture the spirit and dynamism of the Hellenistic style.

Photography Credits

Index

Abdalonymus (king, Sidon), *134*
Abu Simbel (Egypt), 79, *79*
Abu-Sir (Egypt), *35*
Abydos (Egypt), *75–77*
Achaemenid dynasty (Persia), 106
Achilles, 92, *102*, 106
Acropolis (Athens), 98, 116
Aesculapius, *155*
Afghanistan, *128, 129,* 132
agriculture, in ancient Egypt, 22, 30, *30, 31*
Ahmose (pharoah), 46
Ahmose (queen, Egypt), *43,* 46
Akhenaten (Amenhotep IV; pharaoh), 57–68, 77, 78
  Nefertiti, queen to, *53*
  religion of, 52
  statues of, *52*
  wines of, *31*
Akhetaten, *see* Tell-el-Amarna
Alexander I (king, Macedon), 95
Alexander the Great (Alexander III; king, Macedon), 89–93, 164–166
  at battle of Gaugamela, 116, *116,* 118
  at battle of Granicus, 104, 106, 108
  at battle of Issus, 112–115
  becomes king of Macedon, 103
  cities founded by, 144
  confrontation with Darius, 112
  death of, 130
  deification of, 126–129
  dispute between Philip II (Alexander's father) and, 99–102
  funeral of, 134
  in India, 121
  interpretations of, 96, 131
  in Makran desert, 125
  as pharaoh, 88, 89–90
  portraits and statues of, *96, 98, 100, 104, 112, 114, 118, 119, 124, 134*
  proskynesis (kneeling) before, 119–120
  Sardes captured by, *105*
  successors to, 136, *136,* 137
Alexander IV (king, Macedon), 136
Alexander Balas (king, Syria), *153, 158*
Alexander Sarcophagus, *134*
Alexandria (Egypt), 90
  Alexander buried at, 134, 137
  as center of Hellenistic civilization, 138–142
Alexandria (name of seventeen cities), 90, 120
Alexandria-in-Arachosia (Kandahar; Afghanistan), 132
Alexandria-the-Farthest (Asia), 120
Altar of Zeus and Athena (Pergamon), 142, 154
Amazons (mythical), *130*
Amenemmes (pharaoh), 39
Amenemmes II (pharaoh), 42
Amen-her-kopshef (prince, Egypt), *39*
Amenhotep I (pharaoh), *43*
Amenhotep II (pharaoh), *46,* 86
Amenhotep III (pharaoh), 52, 57, 70
  art created under, 58, *80*
  statues of, 46
Amenhotep IV, *see* Akhenaten
Amon (deity), *42, 69,* 129
  Akhenaten's rejection of, 57
  Alexander's sacrifice to, *114*
  Hatshepsut as daughter of, *46*
  priesthood of, 52, 54, 58, 68, 77–79, 83
  procession of Karnak for, *80*
  Re merged with, 72
  shrine at Siwa to, 89, 116
  statue of, *87*
Amon-Re (dual deity), *62,* 72
  ram-headed sphinxes for, *69*

temple-palace of (Karnak), *65*
Amphipolis (Macedon), *94*
Amu (Asiatics; people), *39*
Amu Darya River (Oxus; Asia), *101*
Andromache (mythical), 92
animals
  in Egyptian measurement system, 147
  as gods, in ancient Egypt, 72, *74–75, 77*
Ankhesenamon (Ankhesenpaaten; pharaoh), 68, 70–77
Antigonus Gonatas (king, Macedon), 136, 137, 157
  court at Pella of, 153
  deposed by Pyrrhus, 158
Antigonus the One-Eyed (king, Macedon), 136, 137
Antioch (Seleucid Empire), 150, 164
Antioch (name of sixteen cities), 144
Antioch-on-the-Orontes (Seleucid Empire), 150
Antiochus I (Soter; king, Seleucid Empire), *150*
Antiochus II (Theos; king, Seleucid Empire), *150*
Antiochus III (the Great; king, Seleucid Empire), 137, *152*
  Jews under, 147–150
Antiochus IV (king, Seleucid Empire), 150–152, *152,* 164
Antiochus V (king, Seleucid Empire), *153*
Antiochus VII (king, Seleucid Empire), *158*
Antipater, 103, 104, 116
  Cassander, son of, 134–137
anti-Semitism, 140
Antony, Mark, 148
Apamea, Treaty of, 137
Aphlad (deity), *159*
Aphrodite (deity), *165*
Apis (deity), *75,* 90, 134, *166*
Apollo (deity), *132, 150*
  oracle of (Didyma), *107*
Apophis (mythical), 74
Arachne (legendary), 146
Archelaus (king, Macedon), 95
Archimedes, 148, *148*
Aristotle, 95, *96*
armies
  of ancient Egypt, 40, *40, 41,* 46–52, 57, *62*
  Macedonian, 95–118, 120–129
  see also wars
Arrhidaeus, *see* Philip III Arrhidaeus
Arrian, 104, 108, 129
Arsinoë (queen, Egypt), 138, 158
art
  Akhenaten's changes in, 57, 58
  in Egypt, under Ptolemies, 140
  Greco-Oriental, 132, *132*
  Hellenistic, 160, *160–161*
Artemis (deity), 129
  temple of (Sardes), *105*
Asiatics (Amu; people), *39*
Asoka (king, India), 132
Assos (Greece), *102*
Assyrian Empire, 88
astronomy, 141
Aswan High Dam (Egypt), *10,* 145
Aten (deity), 52, 57, 58
Athena (deity), *132,* 147
  Altar to (Pergamon), 154
Athens (Greece)
  decline of, 153–156
  in Persian Wars, 95–99
  philosophers of, 156–157
Attalid dynasty (Pergamon), 154, *156,* 164
Attalus I (king, Pergamon), *157*
Attalus III (king, Pergamon), 164
Attalus, 99, 103
Atum (deity), *65,* 72
Aureomycin (antibiotic), 62
autarky (self-sufficiency), 157
Avaris (Egypt), 42
Ay (pharaoh), *57,* 77
Azara Herm (portrait of Alexander), *100*

Baboons, domestication in Egypt of, *74*
Babylon

Alexander's conquest of, 116
  coins of, *124, 130*
  Hanging Gardens of, *121*
  South Palace of, *101*
Bactria (ancient kingdom), *129,* 132
Bagoas, 118
Bamian Valley (Afghanistan), *128*
Barsine (princess, Persia; wife of Alexander), 126
Bastet (deity), 74
Beas (Hyphasis) River (India), 121
beer, in ancient Egypt, 30
Begram (Afghanistan), 147
Bergama, *see* Pergamon
Bion of Borysthenes, 157
Black Land (name for Egypt), *10*
block statues, *32*
Blue Nile River (Africa), 22
boats, in ancient Egypt, *18, 38, 40*
Book of the Dead, *38,* 82
Bouchard, Captain, 10
bread, in ancient Egypt, 30
Breasted, J.H., 36, 58
Bubastis (Egypt), 74
Bucephalus (Alexander's horse), *96, 104*
Buddhism, 132
Byblos, temple of (Phoenicia), *113*

Caesar, Julius, 138, 148, *149*
Caesarion (Ptolemy XVI; pharaoh), *149*
calendars, in ancient Egypt, 18
Callisthenes, 93, 120
canals
  in ancient Egypt, *16*
  linking Nile with Red Sea, *140*
Cappadocia (ancient kingdom), *109*
carpentry, in ancient Egypt, *61*
Carter, Howard, 68
Carthage, *148,* 164
Cassander, 134–137
cats, domestication in Egypt of, *74, 75*
Calaenae (Turkey), *105*
Chaeronea (Greece), *94*
  battle of, 95
Champollion, Jean-François, 10–17
Chandragupta (king, India), 132
chariots
  in ancient Egypt, *40,* 46
  at battle of Gaugamela, 116, 118
Chaucer, Geoffrey, 132
Cheops (Khufu; Egyptian tyrant), 34
Christianity, 165
chronology, in ancient Egypt, 10–18
Cleopatra VII (queen, Egypt), 138, 148, *149*
Cleopatra (daughter of Philip II), 103
Cleopatras (queens, Egypt), 138
Cleopatra Thea (queen, Syria), *158*
cleruchies (grants to mercenaries), 145
Clitus, 104
Coenus, 121
coins
  of Alexander's successors, *136*
  Babylonian, *124*
  decadrachma, *130*
  of Egypt under Ptolemies, 138, *138*
  Greco-Indian, 147
  Hellenistic, *93–95*
  of Pergamon, *156*
  Roman, *148*
  silver, abandoned by Athens, 156
Colossi of Memnon (Egypt), 46
commerce, of ancient Egypt, 10, 39
Companion Cavalry (Macedonian army unit), 106, 114, 118
contraception, in ancient Egypt, 62
cosmetics, in ancient Egypt, 50, *50, 51*
cosmology, in ancient Egypt, 72
Craterus, 98, 121, *128,* 129
Crates, 157
Crete, commerce between ancient Egypt and, 39
Croesus (king, Sardes), *105*
Ctesibius, 140
currency
  of Egypt, under Ptolemies, 138, *138*
  see also coins

Cynics (Dog Philosophers), 157
Cyrus the Great (king, Persia), 112, *127*

Dandarah (Egypt), *142, 143*
Darius I (king, Persia), 95, *127*
Darius III (king, Persia), 100, 106, *119,* 137
  at battle of Gaugamela, 116, *116,* 118
  at battle of Issus, 112–115, *112*
death
  Egyptian beliefs relating to, 32, 36, 60
  funeral customs in ancient Egypt and, 84, *84–86*
  Opening of the Mouth rite of, 57
  Weighing of the Heart ritual of, 38, *38, 72*
decadrachma (coin), *130*
Deir-el-Bahri (Egypt), *46*
  Hatsheput's temple at, *42,* 43
  mummies hidden in, 86
  mummies looted in, 87
Deir-el-Medina (Egypt), *75*
Demeter, sanctuary of (Pergamon), 154
Demetrius I Soter (king, Seleucid Empire), *153*
Demetrius of Phalerum, 131
Demetrius Poliorcetes (king, Macedon), 132, 136, *136,* 137
Demosthenes, *93,* 95, 98, 104
demotic (ancient Egyptian script), 20
Didyma (Caria), *107*
Diocletian (emperor, Rome), *149*
Diogenes the Cynic, *96*
Dionysis, 150
Dionysus (deity), *93*
Djet (pharaoh), *23*
Djoser (pharaoh), 26
  Step Pyramid of, *24, 25, 26–27*
Drypetis (princess, Persia), 126
Dura-Europos (Mesopotamia), *159*

Early Dynastic Period (3200–2780 B.C.; Egypt), *14*
Ecbatana (Persia), 116
Edfu (Egypt), temple to Horus at, *140*
Egypt, ancient
  under Alexander, 88, 89–90, 92, *114,* 116
  First Intermediate Period of, 36–39
  hieroglyphics of, 10–17, 20
  legends about Alexander in, 100, 130
  linen invented in, 146
  maps of, *14, 15, 19*
  Middle Kingdom of, 39–42
  mythology of, 24
  New Kingdom of, 46–86
  Old Kingdom of, 34
  periods and kingdoms of, *14–15*
  under Ptolemies, 134–142, *138,* 145
  Rome and Seleucid Empire at war over, 152, 164
  Second Intermediate Period of, 42–46
  Twenty-fifth Dynasty of, 87–88
  Two Lands, name of, 9
  unification of, 25–26
  weights and measures in, 147, *147*
Eighteenth Dynasty (Egypt), *42,* 46–77
Emergence of the Fields (Egypt), 18, 22
Empiricists, 142
Enkhesenamon (queen, Egypt), *49*
Ephesus (Caria), 108, *109*
Ephippus, 126–129
Epicurus, 156–157
Epirus (ancient kingdom), 103
Eratosthenes of Cyrene, 141
Erdek (Turkey), *164*
Eros (deity), 165
Euclid, 141
Eumenes II (king, Pergamon), 154
Euphrates River (Asia), *101, 116*

family
  in ancient Egypt, 48
  in Macedon, 99
Fars (Persia), 124
Fayum (Egypt), 39–42, 74
Fields of Yalu (mythical), *30*
Fifth Dynasty (Egypt), *35*
First Intermediate Period (2258–2040 B.C., Egypt), *14,* 36–39

flabellum (ceremonial fan), *58*
Flamininus, Titus Quinctius, 164
flax, 146, *146*
flooding of Nile, 22
food, in ancient Egypt, 30, *61*
Fourth Dynasty (Egypt), *26,* 27
funeral customs
  in ancient Egypt, 84, *84–86*
  see also death

Galatians (Gauls), *150,* 154, *157*
Gandhara (ancient kingdom), 132, *132*
Ganymede (mythical), *132, 166*
Gaugamela, battle of, 116, *116,* 118
Gauls (Galatians), *150,* 154, *157*
Gaza (Phoenicia), 115
Géramb, Baron François Ferdinand de, 10
Giza (Egypt)
  pyramids of, *26, 27, 35, 114*
  Sphinx, *26*
gold
  in ancient Egypt, 52
  burying with mummies of, 84, 86
  in coins, *93, 94*
  in Hellenistic civilization, 162, *162–163*
  in Tutankhamon's tomb, 68, 70
  used as currency by Alexander, 116
Gonatas, *see* Antigonus Gonatas
Gordium (Phrygia), *109,* 112
Goreme (Cappadocia), *109*
government
  in ancient Egypt, during New Kingdom, 70
  in cities conquered by Alexander, 108
  in Persian empire, 106
graffiti, 10
Granicus, battle of, 104, 106, 108
grave robbing, 84, 86, 87
Great Hypostyle Hall (Egypt), 69
Greco-Oriental art, 132, *132*
Greece, ancient
  under Alexander, 119
  Alexander's integration of Persia with, 126
  Asia Minor under influence of, 144–145
  battle of Granicus and, 104, 106, 108
  commerce between Egypt and, 10
  decline of, 153–156
  Egyptian gods and, 88
  Egypt influenced by, 138–142
  expansion of, under Alexander, 90–91
  Indian art influenced by, 132, *132*
  interpretations of Alexander in, 130–131
  linen in, 146
  in Persian Wars, 95–99
  wars between Rome and, 164
  see also Hellenistic civilization
gymnasia, 144

Habiru (people), 64
Hadda (Asia), *132*
Halicarnassus (Caria), 108, *109*
Hanging Gardens of Babylon, *121*
Hapy (deity), *18*
Hathor (deity), *49,* 65, *142*
Hatshepsut (regent; pharaoh), 54, 57, *69*
  Amon as father of, *46*
  temple at Deir-el-Bahri built under, *42,* 43
Hector (mythical), 92
hedonism, in ancient Egypt, 36
Heiro (king, Syracuse), 148
Helicon (mountain, Greece), *166*
Heliopolis (Egypt), *69,* 72
Hellenistic civilization
  after Alexander, 131
  Alexandria as center of, 138–140
  art of, 160, *160–161*
  in Asia, 147
  in Asia Minor, 144–145
  decline of, 153–158, 164
  gold decoration in, 162, *162–163*
  writing of, *141*
  see also Greece, ancient
Hephaestion, 106, 114, 126, 130
Hera (deity), 154
Heracles (deity), 95, 121, 129, *150*

Heraclides, 156
Herihor (priest), 88
Herodotus
  on Egypt, 10, 17, 32, 34
  in Macedon, 95
  on Persian army, 106
  on Persian customs, 116
Herophilus, 142
Hesire, *33*
hetaroi (Macedonian nobles), 93
hieratic (ancient Egyptian script), 20, *20*
hieroglyphics, 20
  Rosetta stone, key to, 10–17, *20*
  see also writing
Hieronymus (king, Syracuse), *148*
Hindu Kush (mountains, Asia), *128–130*
Hipparchus of Nicaea, 141
Hittites (people), 64, 70–79
Horemheb (pharaoh), *65,* 7.7–78
Hor-Si-Hor, 145
Horus (name of two deities), *23,* 24, *55, 72, 138*
  in Re-Harakhte, *73*
  temple of (Edfu), *140*
  see also Throne of Horus
Hyksos (people), *40,* 42–46
Hymn to the Aten (Akhenaten), 52, 58
Hyphasis (Beas) River (India), 121

Imhotep, *25,* 27
incest, in Egyptian royal families, 48, 138
India
  Alexander in, 120–121, *127, 130*
  Greek influences on art of, 132, *132*
Indus River (India), 121, *128,* 130
Inherkhau, *55*
Inundation of Nile, 18, 22
Ipsus, battle of, 136, 137
Iran, *see* Persia
Ishtar (deity), *121*
Isis (deity), 24, *72,* 145
Isocrates, 131
Issus, battle of, 112–115, *112*

Jacob (biblical), 30
Jason (Joshua), 150
Jerusalem, 150
jewelry, Hellenistic, 162, *162–163*
Jews
  in Egypt, 138–140
  in Hellenistic civilization, 147
  Maccabee revolt of, 137, 150, *153,* 164, 165
Joseph (biblical), 46
Joshua (Jason), 150
Judaea, 147, *153*
Judicial Papyrus of Turin, 82

ka (spiritual double), *57,* 60, 82, *84*
Kadesh (Egypt), 57
  battle of, *40,* 78, 79
Kaemhesit, *33*
Kandahar (Alexandria-in-Arachosia; Afghanistan), 132
Kaoshan (Afghanistan), *129*
Karnak (Egypt)
  Avenue of the Rams in, 69
  Karomama's chapel at, 87
  statue of Akhenaten in, *52*
  temples of, *43,* 54, *65,* 78, *80*
Karomama (queen, Egypt), *87*
Kay (scribe), *20*
Khafre (pharaoh), *26*
Khafre pyramid, 27
Khnum (deity), *72*
Khufu (Cheops; Egyptian tyrant), 34
Khufu pyramid, 27
Koine (dialect), 138
Kom Ombo (Egypt), *138, 147*
Kush (ancient desert kingdom), *19,* 88

Labyrinth of Knossos, temple of Amenemes III as prototype of, 42
Laenas, Popillius, 152
Lake Nasser (Egypt), *10,* 79
Lake Victoria (Africa), *16*

Late Kingdom (715–332 B.C.; Egypt), 15
League of Corinth, 95, 104
Lebanon, 39, 52, 61
Leochares, 94
Libyans (people), 79, 80
linen, invention of, 146, 146
Lion of Amphipolis, 94
Lower Egypt, 19, 25–26
Luxor (Egypt), 80, 114
Lysimachus of Thrace (king, Macedon), 136, 136, 137
Lysippus, 100

Ma'at (deity), 73
ma'at (Egyptian belief), 35, 36, 38
Maccabaeus, Judas 150
Maccabees, 137, 150, 153, 164, 165
Macedon (Macedonia)
  after Alexander, 131 137
  Alexander as king of, 103–125
  Alexander's integration of Persia with Greece and, 126, 129
  long march of armies of, under Alexander, 100, 101–102
  in Persian Wars, 93–99
  under Roman domination, 152–153
  wars between Rome and, 158–164
Maeander River (Asia), 105
Magadha (ancient kingdom), 121
magic, in ancient Egypt, 62, 62
Makran desert (Persia), 125
Manetho, 140
marriage
  in ancient Egypt, 48, 138
  polygamous, in Macedon, 99
Marsden, E.W., 118
Mauryan Empire (Asia), 132, 137
Mausolus (king, Caria), 109
Maya (Tutankhamon's Overseer of Works), 68–70
Mazaeus, 116
measurement, in ancient Egypt, 147, 147
medicine
  in ancient Egypt, 25, 62, 62, 63
  in Hellenistic Egypt, 141–142
Medinet Habu (temple, Egypt), 80, 82
Memnon, 106–108
Memphis (Egypt), 72
  Alexander buried at, 134
  Alexander's conquest of, 114
  necropolises of, 35
  Ptah, god of, 36
  Sphinx of, 26
Menander (king, India), 147
Menes (Narmer; first pharaoh), 23, 25, 26
Menkaure (pharaoh), 26
Menkaure pyramid, 27
Menmaare Seti-Merenptah, see Seti I
Mentuhotep II (pharaoh), 36, 39
mercenaries, 145–147
Merenptah (pharaoh), 79–80
Mereruka, 35
Meresankh, 32
Meroe (Egypt), 87
Mesopotamia, Alexander in, 116, 116
Meteora plain (Thessaly), 91
Midas (king, mythical), 112
Middle Kingdom (2040–1786 B.C.; Egypt), 14, 38, 39–42
Mitri, 35
monogamy, in ancient Egypt, 48
Mount Pangaeus (Thrace), 94
Mouseion (Museum; Alexandria, Egypt), 140, 141
mummies
  preparation of, 84, 84–85
  protection of, 86–87
  scientific study of, 63
  see also death
Murray, Gilbert, 148
Myron of Pergamon, 160
mythology of ancient Egypt
  cosmology in, 72

Osiris, Seth and Isis myth, 24
  see also religion

Nakht, tomb of, 48
Napoleon Bonaparte, 10
Narmer (Menes; first pharaoh), 23, 25, 26
Nasser, Lake (Egypt), 10, 79
navies, of Alexander, 106, 121, 125
Nearchus, 125, 128
Nebkheprure, see Tutankhamon
Necho (Assyrian king of Egypt), 88
Nectanebo II (pharaoh), 90, 100, 130
Nefertari (queen, Egypt), 18, 79
Nefertiti (queen, Egypt), 52, 53, 57, 64–65
Nekhebet (deity), 58
nemes (headdress), 24
Neoptolemus (mythical), 92
Nephthys (deity), 72
New Kingdom (1570–1085 B.C.; Egypt), 15, 38, 46–86
Nike (deity), 124
Nile River (Africa), 10, 16, 19
  Napoleon's expedition to, 10
  narrow valley of, 17–22
  river boats on, 18
Nimaasted (scribe), 33
Nimrud Dağ, 150
Nineteenth Dynasty (Egypt), 40, 78–79
Nubia (Egypt), 19, 60, 79, 88
  conquered by Sesostris III, 39
  gold mined in, 52, 83
  pyramids in, 87
Nut (deity), 57

Old Kingdom (2780–2258 B.C.; Egypt), 14, 34–36
Olympia (Greece), 94
Olympias (queen, Macedon; mother of Alexander), 103, 134, 158
  exile of, 99
  legends and rumors about, 92–93
Opening of the Mouth (funeral rite), 57
Osiris (mythical god-king), 57, 70, 72
  in beliefs about death, 30, 58
  commoners as, 38
  merged into Serapis, 134
  myth of, 24
  pharaohs as, 27
  power shared between Re and, 34
  Rameses III's sculptures to, 69
Osorkon I (pharaoh), 87
Oxus River (Amu Darya; Asia), 101, 144

Palermo stone, 20
Palestine, 137, 142–144
papyrus, 20, 21, 22, 142
parchment, 142
Parmenion, 103, 104, 115–118
Parthians, 137
Pasargadae (Persia), 124, 127
Patroclus, 106
Pausanias, 103
Pella (Macedon), 91–93, 98
  Macedonian capital in, 95
Pepi I (pharaoh), 41
Pepi II (pharaoh), 34–36
Perdiccas (regent, Macedon), 136
Pergamon (Asia Minor), 153–156
  as center of Hellenistic civilization, 142, 154
  portraits of Alexander from, 96, 112
Pericles, 160
Persepolis (Persia), 116, 124, 127
Perseus (king, Macedon), 153, 158
Persia (Iran)
  after Alexander, 142
  under Alexander, 119
  Alexander's integration of Greece and Macedon with, 126, 129
  in battle of Gaugamela, 116, 116, 118
  in battle of Granicus, 104, 106, 108
  in battle of Issus, 112–115
  conquered by Alexander, 100, 124
  in early wars with Macedon, 93–99
  Egypt dominated by, 88, 90
  Hellenistic jewelry inspired by, 162

Sardes captured by Alexander from, 105
Persian Gulf, 101, 121
Persian Wars, 93–99
Petamenopet (scribe), 32
Petrie, Sir Flinders, 22
Pewera, 86
pharaohs
  Alexander, 89–90, 92, 114
  early non-Egyptian, 87–88
  incest in royal families of, 48
  Menes (first), 25
  Ptolemies, 134–141, 145
  pyramids built by, 34
  see also names of individual pharaohs and individual dynasties
Pharos lighthouse (Egypt), 140
Philae (Egypt), 145
Philetaeros, 156
Philip II (king, Macedon), 91, 93–103, 93–95, 153
  Demetrius of Phalerum on, 131
Philip III Arrhidaeus (king, Macedon), 102, 131, 134, 136, 136
Philip V (king, Macedon), 158–164
Philippeion, 94
Philo, 140
philosophers
  in Alexandria, 140
  in Athens, 156–157
Philotas, 118
Philoxenos of Eratria, 112
Phoenicia, 144
  Alexander's conquest of, 115
  temple of Byblos in, 113
Piankhi (pharaoh), 87–88
Pindar, 95
Plato, 140
Pliny the Elder, 10, 146
Plutarch, 130
Polybius, 150–152
polygamy, in Macedonian royal family, 99
Polyhymnia, 160
Pompeii (Italy), 112
Pompey's Pillar (Egypt), 149
Porus (king, Punjab), 121, 130
Poseidon (deity), 136
pottery, (in ancient Egypt), 60
Priene (Greece), 103
Processional Way (Babylon), 121
proskynesis (Persian custom), 119–120
Psamtik (Assyrian ruler of Egypt), 88
Ptah (deity), 36, 72, 73
Ptolemies (pharaohs), 136–141, 138, 145
  Antiochus III's defeat of, 152
  Rome as protector of, 152, 164
Ptolemy I (pharaoh), 134 137, 138
Ptolemy II Philadelphus (pharaoh), 137–140, 140, 158
Ptolemy V Epiphanes (pharaoh), 20, 142, 144
Ptolemy VIII Euergetes (pharaoh), 147
Ptolemy XVI (Caesarion; pharaoh), 149
Punt (ancient African country), 39, 43, 54
Pydna, battle of, 153
pyramids
  at Abu-sir, 35
  of Amenemmes III, 42
  building of, 34
  Djoser's Step Pyramid, 24, 25, 26–27
  of Giza, 26, 35, 114
  in Nubia, 87
Pyramid Texts, 82
Pyrrhus (king, Epirus), 158

Rameses I (pharaoh), 78
Rameses the Great (Rameses II; pharaoh), 69, 80
  Abu Simbel temples built under, 79
  at battle of Kadesh, 40, 78–79
  mummy of, 63, 87
  temple of (Abydos), 75–77
Rameses III (pharaoh), 69, 80–82, 82, 83
Ramases IV (pharaoh), 82
Rameses VI (pharaoh), 21, 68, 86
Ramesseum, 36, 82
Ramose (pharaoh), 84
Rasuls family, 87

Re (deity), 68, 72
  Amon merged with, 57
  mythology of, *74*
  power shared between Osiris and, 34
  pyramids and temples dedicated to, *35*
Red Land (desert, Africa), 10
Re-Harakhte (dual deity), *73, 147*
Reherka, *32*
religion
  of Akhenaten, 52, 57, 58
  Alexander's deification and, 126–129
  in ancient Egypt, 36, 38, 72
  in ancient Egypt, animals in, 74, *74–75, 77*
  Buddhism, 132
  in divisions among Jews, 150
  Hellenistic civilization's impact on, 165
  of Hyksos, 42–46
  problems of Jews in Hellenistic civilization and, 147
  proskynesis, Persian ritual, 119–120
  Serapsi cult, 134–138
  see also death
Reshef (deity), *113*
river boats, in ancient Egypt, *18*
Rome, ancient (Roman Empire)
  Antiochus III defeated by, 137
  commerce between Egypt and, 10
  decline of Hellenism and, 148, *148,* 164–165
  linen in, 146
  Seleucid Empire at war with, 150, 152, *152*
  wars between Macedon and, 153, 158–164
Rosetta stone, 10–17, *20*
Roxane (princess, Sogdiana; wife of Alexander), 118, 131, 136

Sacred Band (Theban army unit), 95
Sacred Way to Delphi, *95*
Saites (Assyrian ruler of Egypt), 88
Sanderson, John, 10
Saqqara (Egypt)
  animal cults in, 74, *75*
  Djoser's Step Pyramid at, *24, 25,* 26–27
  scenes from, *31, 40*
  statue of Nimaasted in, *33*
  tombs of Ty and Mitri in, *35*
Sarang Pass (Asia), *101*
Sardes (ancient kingdom), *105*
satraps (persian governors), 106
science
  in ancient Egypt, 10, *25*
  in Hellenistic civilization, art and, 160
  in Hellenistic Egypt, 141–142
Scorpion (ruler in Nile Valley), 22
scribes, in ancient Egypt, *20,* 32, *33*
sculptors, in ancient Egypt, *35*
Sea Peoples, 79, 80
Second Intermediate Period (1786–1570 B.C.; Egypt), *15,* 42–46
Sekhmet (deity), *73*
Seleucia (name of nine cities), 144
Seleucid dynasty (Seleucid Empire), 137, 144–145, 147, *150*
Seleucid Empire, 150, *152*
  after Alexander, 136, 137
  Sardes under, *105*
  wars between Rome and, 150–152, 164
Seleucus I Nicator (king, Seleucid Empire), *107,* 144, *150, 151*
  in contention for succession to Alexander, 136, 137, 142
Semiramis (queen, Babylon), 125
Seneb, *33*
Senedjem, *30*
Senmut, 54
Sen-nefer, tomb of, *18*
Sequenenre the Brave, 46
Serapis (composite deity), 134–138, 149
serekh, 23
Sesostris I (pharaoh), *36*
Sesostris III (pharaoh), 39
Seth (mythical), 24, 46, *55*
Seti I (pharaoh), *49,* 78, 87
  Great Hypostyle Hall built under, *69*
  tomb of, *70*

Seven Wonders of the Ancient World
  Alter of Zeus and Athena (Pergamon), 142, 154
  Hanging Gardens of Babylon, *121*
  Halicarnassus (Caria), 108, *109*
  pyramids of Giza, *26*
shaduf (bucket), 18
Shatby (Egypt), *114*
shawabits (mummiform figures), 60
Sheshonq (pharaoh), 87
Shu (mythical), 72
Shubilulliuma (king, Hittites), 70–77
Sidon (ancient kingdom), *98, 134*
Sikander (legendary name for Alexander), 100, 130
Siwa (Libya), 89, 92, 116
  Alexander's request to be buried at, 134, 137
Smenkhkare (pharaoh), *54,* 64–68
Sobek (deity), 74, *138, 147*
Sobekhotep III (pharaoh), *39*
Sogdiana, 118, *129*
Song of the Harper, 36
Sostratus of Cnidus, 140
South Palace (Babylon), *101*
Sparta (Greece), 95, 104, 116, 126, 158
sphinxes
  of Giza, *26*
  of Memphis, *26*
  ram-headed, *69*
Spitamenes, 137
Step Pyramid (Saqqara), *24, 25,* 26–27
Stoics, 157, 164
"Story of Two Brothers, The," 50
Susa (Persia), 116, *124,* 126, *127*
Syracuse, siege of, *148*
Syria, 39, 52, 57, 113
  Seleucid Empire reduced to, 137

Tanagra figures, *153, 165*
Tarn, W.W., 165–166
Tarsus (Turkey), 112
Taurus Mountains (Turkey), *101, 102*
Tefnut (mythical), 72
Telephus (demi-god), 154
Telesphorus, *155*
Tell-el-Amarna (Akhetaten; Egypt), 64
  as capital, 52, 57, 58
  statues of Akhenaten in, *52*
Temple of Amon (Karnak), *43,* 54
Thais, 116
Thebes (Egypt), *36*
  Akhenaten's abandonment of, 57
  Alexander's destruction of, 104, 108
  army of, 95
  as capital, *42*
  grave robbing in, 86
  rebellion in, 46
  return of capital to, by Tutankhamon, 68
  tomb of Nakht in, *48*
Thessaly (Greece)
  jewelry of, *162–163*
  Meteora plain of, *91*
Third Dynasty (Egypt), 26
Third Intermediate Period (1085–715 B.C.; Egypt), *15*
Thoth (deity), *38, 75*
Thrace, Mount Pangaeus of, *94*
Throne of Horus, 10, *72,* 134, 137
  see also Horus; pharaohs
Thutmose I (pharaoh), *43,* 46, 54, 57
Thutmose III (pharaoh), *46,* 54–57, 78, 87
Thutmose (sculptor), *53*
Ti (queen, Egypt), 80–82
Tigris River (Asia), 116, *116*
Tiy (queen, Egypt), 57
tomb robbing, 84, 86, 87
Troy (Greece), 106
Tutankhamon (pharaoh), *49, 56–58,* 68–70, 77
Twelfth Dynasty (Egypt), 39, 42
Twentieth Dynasty (Egypt), 80–86
Twenty-second Dynasty (Egypt), 87
Twenty-fifth Dynasty (Egypt), 87–88
Two Lands (name of ancient Egyptian kingdom), 9, *72*
  first unification of, 25

Nekhebet and Wadjet symbols of, *58*
  reseparation of, 83
  reunification of, 39
  see also Egypt, ancient
Ty, 35
Tyche (deity), 131
Tyre (Phoenicia), *113,* 115, 116, *116*
Upper Egypt, *17,* 19, 25–26
ushabits (mummiform figures), 60

Vardar River (Macedonia), *91*
Victoria, Lake (Africa), 16
viticulture (wine making), in ancient Egypt, *31*

Wadjet (deity), *58*
wars
  of ancient Egypt, 40, *40,* 46–57, 78–80
  battle of Gaugamela, 116, *116,* 118
  battle of Granicus, 104, 106, 108
  battle of Issus, 112–115, *112*
  between Rome and Macedon, 153, 158–164
  between Rome and Seleucid Empire, 150, 152
  of Pergamon, 142
  Persian, 93–99
Weighing of the Heart (ritual), 38, *38,* 72
weights and measures, in ancient Egypt, 147, *147*
wigs, in ancient Egypt, 50, *50*
wines, in ancient Egypt, *31*
Winged Victory of Samothrace, *166*
women
  adornment of, in ancient Egypt, 50, *50, 51*
  in ancient Egypt, 17, 48
  of Eighteenth Dynasty (Egypt), *42*
  as rulers of ancient Egypt, 54, 70–77
writing
  in ancient Egypt, 20, *20, 21,* 22
  of Hellenistic civilization, 141
  see also hieroglyphics

Xenophon, 100, 106, 112
Xerxes (king, Persia) 95, 98, *127*

zenet (game), 55
Zeno of Cyprus, 157, 166
Zeus (deity), *132, 166*
  Alter to (Pergamon), 142, 154
Zeus-Amon (dual deity), 92, *138*